STRENGTH AND PHYSIQUE

VOLUME ONE: THE ARTICLES

by James Chan, NSCA-CPT

STRENGTH AND PHYSIQUE

VOLUME ONE: THE ARTICLES

by James Chan, NSCA-CPT

Published 2008

Manufactured in the United States of America.

About the Author

James Chan works as a police officer for the University of California Police Department in San Francisco. In addition to his patrol duties, James is also a defensive tactics instructor for the department. As a hobby, James conducts personal training off-duty, specializing in strength training for law enforcement and physique enhancement for the general population. He is certified through the National Strength and Conditioning Association and may be reached at strengthandphysique@yahoo.com. For more information on his services, visit his website at www.strengthandphysique.com

To tap into his insights on strength training and bodybuilding, visit his blog at:
www.strengthandphysique.blogspot.com

TABLE OF CONTENTS

XVI. The Six Factors of Hypertrophy

Recommended Reading

INTRODUCTION

Psst!

I'll let you in on a little secret: you really don't need a personal trainer. I know this, because I *am* a personal trainer. All of the information that you need to build a rock hard body is out there in bits and pieces in books, magazines and the internet. People working out at the gym can give you useful advice from time to time.

The problem is that you have to sift through a lot of misinformation to get to the truth. If you're new to bodybuilding or physique training and you don't know how to tell the truth from misinformation, then you might as well hire a well-qualified personal trainer to guide you.

But if you are smart, disciplined and willing to spend *years* in the gym researching and testing out various training methods, then you don't need a trainer.

What you have in your hands is a compilation of my training articles that I've written for various sources, such as T-Nation.com, Fitness and Physique magazine, MindandMuscle.net and my own site www.strengthandphysique.com. The articles are primarily geared towards bodybuilding enthusiasts and for those who enjoy weight training to sculpt a better physique.

I come from an old school bodybuilding philosophy, where if you lift heavy and intelligently focus your efforts, then you'll build an impressive muscular physique. In these articles you'll find many of the battle-tested techniques and strategies that have worked for my clients and for me. You don't have to sift through a lot of misinformation and spend years testing out various programs. This compilation of articles comprehensively covers bodybuilding training and will shortcut your muscle quest from years to months.

I always enjoy hearing from readers of my articles, so feel free to send me an email on your progress: strengthandphysique@yahoo.com.

I. Establish Your Goal as a Bodybuilder: Symmetry or Bulk?

The first thing you need to establish is what your goal is as a bodybuilder. Are you looking for overall muscle mass? Or are you looking to put on muscle in specific body parts? Is your goal "symmetry" or is it "bulk?"

The concept of muscle bulk is the idea a trainee gains as much muscle as possible throughout his body, regardless of how it looks overall. This concept is also known as "power bodybuilding," whereby you develop muscle mass through the use of heavy compound movements (such as the bench press, deadlifts and squats) and supplementary bodybuilding movements (barbell curls, lateral raises, etc).

The heavy compound movements are used to develop as much muscle mass over as many body parts as possible. This is analogous to using a shotgun to destroy your target. It's not pretty, but it gets the job done.

There is a problem with the power bodybuilding method: if you want to look good naked and appeal to the opposite sex, then this method alone will not give you that look. Because heavy compound movements such the bench press, back squat and deadlifts are used, the trainer develops a hunched over look, much like a caveman.

While their overall mass is impressive, their overall physiques are not. Power bodybuilders have massive trapezius development, which detracts from the wide shoulder look sought after by bodybuilders. Because of their emphasis on heavy benching, power bodybuilders also have bulbous looking chest muscles, making them looking like they have breasts.

Heavy squatting and overeating by power bodybuilders builds their waist. Despite their well-developed six packs, their guts are distended due to heavy squatting and overeating. This is due to the fact that in order to squat heavy, a power bodybuilder needs to fill his diaphragm with air and expand his waistline in order to create a stable base from which to lift. Heavy squats as well as heavy deadlifts will build and widen the hips, which takes away from the long legged look desired by many bodybuilders, particularly those of smaller stature.

This is not to say power bodybuilding moves should be avoided completely. Movements such as hang cleans and squats can be used to add much needed mass on an ectomorph, and the mass can be sculpted through the use of more targeted bodybuilding movements.

The concept of "muscle symmetry" is the idea a trainee develops muscle in *certain* body parts to create a certain look, an aesthetic that is pleasing to the eye. This aesthetic is the look of the "classical bodybuilder," who seeks to attain lean overall muscularity, broad looking shoulders, a flat narrow waist, and long toned legs. This aesthetic is also known as a "V-taper" or an "X-frame."

The two extreme examples of power bodybuilding and classical bodybuilding are Tom Platz and Steve Reeves. Tom Platz has a thick, dense look to his musculature (bulk), whereas Steve Reeves has a chiseled angular look to his muscles (symmetry). If you were to look at the silhouettes of these two bodybuilders in their prime, you would see a clear distinction between the two. Whereas Platz has a Neanderthal look to his physique (sorry Tom!), Reeves clearly has a physique reminiscent of Greek and Roman sculptures.

The Classical Bodybuilder

For the classical bodybuilder, particular exercises are performed to isolate and develop particular muscles and particular portions of a muscle complex. This method is the antithesis of the power bodybuilding method. Rather than use a "shotgun approach," classical bodybuilders use a targeted approach to muscle building. Strategic muscles are developed to give the overall illusion of size, while the development of other body parts is minimized to obtain the coveted ideal proportions. Classical bodybuilders focus on these areas:

- Broad shoulders, minimal trapezius development

- V-tapered back, with special emphasis on the teres major
- Development of the outer edges of the pectoral muscles
- Small, flat waist
- Narrow hips and minimal glute development
- Long toned legs, with special emphasis on the vastus medialis and calves

For every power bodybuilding movement (which builds mass indiscriminately), there is a corresponding classical bodybuilding movement that helps build muscle in all the right places:

Overall Muscle Builder	Targeted Muscle Builder
Back squats	Front squats, sissy squats, leg extensions
Conventional pull-ups	Sternum pull-ups, side to side pull-ups
Powerlifter's bench press	Neck press
Chest dips on parallel bars	Wide grip dips on V-bars
Deadlifts	Barbell Hack squats
Hang cleans, Power cleans	Wide grip upright barbell rows
Seated close grip cable rows	Lat bar cable rows
Romanian deadlifts	Good mornings, machine leg curls

If you've noticed, arms and calves are not listed in the overall muscle builder category, since arm and calf training are, by definition, targeted movements. You'll also notice that the classical bodybuilding movements are actually more difficult to perform than power bodybuilding movements. This is because with power bodybuilding movements you rely on better leverages to move the weight.

So establish your goal as a bodybuilder: bulk or symmetry? If you're an endomorph or a mesomorph, then focus on classical bodybuilding movements. If you're an ectomorph and are in need of muscle, then focus on power bodybuilding movements.

II. Split Decisions

When figuring out their training routine, most newbie lifters focus solely on exercise selection and how to split up the muscle groups throughout the week. With regards to program design, however, there's more simply than just, "Hey, today is chest, shoulders and triceps." An effective muscle-building program factors in the following:

The Ideal Training Frequency

How often should you train each body part? I'll make it very simple for you: you should train each desired body part 3-4 times per week directly or indirectly. What this means, however, is that each body part needs to be hit 3 times per week, either directly or indirectly, within a three to four-day per week program. This happens to be the optimal range for gaining and maintaining muscle mass. Any more and you will overtrain. Any less and you undertrain.

The Ideal Training Split

With the optimal training frequency established, what is the best training split? Are full body workouts the way to go? Or should you train with split routines, dividing the body arbitrarily? There are advantages to both, so hence both should be used.

With full body routines, each muscle group can be hit every time you workout. So you can easily train each muscle group 3-4 times per week. The more frequently you train, the faster you will gain muscle and the easier it is to maintain your newfound muscle.

There is one problem and that is this: although whole body workouts allow you to train each muscle group more frequently, the number of sets of exercise for each muscle group will be severely limited. For example, if you did 3 exercises per body part at 3 sets for all 8 major muscle groups (chest, back, quadriceps, hamstrings, calves, biceps, triceps, and shoulders), your total workout would be 72 sets at approximately three and half hours long (if you stuck to 1 minute rest periods).

This would be unacceptable (not to mention tiring), since the ideal workout should never go beyond 1 hour. Any longer, and you would be overtraining. To cut down on the number of sets, you would simply choose one exercise for each major body part.

Hence if you were to devote 3 sets of one exercise to each of the 8 major body parts, you would have 24 total sets per workout, and this would fit into the one hour limit. Those who wish to use different exercises for the same muscle group can simply alternate among various exercises from workout to workout.

With a split routine, however, the body is split according the desired muscle groups, and the workout goes according to group by group. The advantage of this is that you can devote more sets to each body part. Greater volume of work induces a greater growth response from your muscles. Plus, you can use more than one exercise per muscle group, which also induces greater growth.

A common split would be and upper body workout alternated with a lower body workout. If you wanted to train specific muscle groups, you could devote an entire workout to each body part.

There is of course a disadvantage to this as well: using a split routine limits how frequently you can train each body part. If you used solely an upper body/lower body split and trained 4 times per week, you would find that you train each muscle only twice a week, one short of the ideal frequency.

There is a way use both split routines and full body routines within one program. Here are two options:

Split A:

Sunday	Monday	Tuesday	Wednesday	Thursday	Friday	Saturday
Full body workout		Full body workout		Lower body workout	Upper body workout	

Split B:

Sunday	Monday	Tuesday	Wednesday	Thursday	Friday	Saturday
Full body workout		Full body workout		Full body workout	Speciali-zation	

Split A gives you the best of both worlds for every body part. You get the required frequency need to gain and maintain muscle, and you get added volume from a split routine. Each body part is stressed three times per week.

Split B extends these benefits even further. Split B allows you to train full body frequently, while specializing in one, two or three body parts. On "Specialization Day," you can focus on a particular muscle group that is lagging in development. For instance, if your calves needed extra development, then your specialization day would focus on calf training. This "calf day" would be in addition to your regular calf training in the 3 full body workouts.

Rotating Exercises

When it comes to exercise selection, most bodybuilders employ an "everything and the kitchen sink "approach. Bodybuilders typically employ anywhere from 3 to 5 exercises for just one body part.

Although multi-angular training has its place, your nervous system would burn out from performing so many exercises for each body part at each session. It is far more productive to perform one exercise per muscle group and rotate among a few different exercises throughout the week.

Let's use the quads as an example:

Monday – Hack Squats
Wednesday – Leg Press
Friday – Front Squats

Simply choose 3 of your favorite exercise for each muscle group and rotate among the three throughout the week. This provides two advantages:

1. Consistency of exercises – you hit each exercise once a week
2. High training frequency – although you rotate exercises, you train each body part at least three times a week

Exercise Selection

For athletes, exercise selection is based on a balance of movements: vertical pressing, vertical pulling, horizontal pressing, horizontal pulling, and so on and so forth. For bodybuilders, however, exercise selection is based on the full hypertrophy of all portions of a muscle.

Bodybuilders can achieve full development of most muscle groups with just 2 carefully selected exercises. On the following page is a chart detailing the dual hypertrophy goals for each muscle group and exercise examples for each goal:

Chest	Target: Upper Chest	Target: Lower Chest
	Exercises: 20° DB press, Guillotine press	Exercises: Wide grip V-bar dips
Back	Target: Latissimus Dorsi	Target: Midback
	Exercises: Pull-ups, Pulldowns	Exercises: Seated cable rows

Deltoids	Target: Lateral Head Exercises: Dumbbell laterals	Target: Posterior Head Exercises: Lying Rear Flyes
Biceps	Target: Both Heads of the Biceps Exercises: Incline Curls	Target: Brachialis Exercises: Preacher curls, Zottman curls
Triceps	Target: Long Head Exercises: Lying EZ-bar extensions	Target: Lateral and Medial Head Exercises: Dips, Pressdowns, Close grip presses
Quadriceps	Target: Vastus Medialis Exercises: Front Squat, Hack Squats, Sissy Squats	Target: Rest of the Quadriceps Exercises: Reverse Lunges, Back Squats (heels raised), Leg Press
Hamstrings	Target: Biceps Femoris Exercises: Leg curls	Target: Semitendinosus and Semimembranosus Exercises: Romanian Deadlifts, Good Mornings
Calves	Target: Gastrocnemius Exercises: Standing Machine Calf Raises, Donkey Calf Raises	Target: Soleus Exercises: Seated Calf Raises

Ideally, a bodybuilder can alternate back and forth between two portions of a muscle group. Here's how a series of deltoid workouts would look throughout the week:

Monday – Wide Grip Upright Rows (Lateral Head Development)
Wednesday – Lying Rear Flyes (Posterior Head Development)
Friday – Swing Laterals (Lateral Head Development)

Take Your Program Design to the Next Level

Now that you understand training frequency and exercise selection, you can take your program to the next level.

Train smart and stay safe.

III. Quad Quest

While most bodybuilding newbies are motivated to pump up their upper bodies, the true hardcore lifter (and masochist) looks forward to blasting his thighs. Want to know who's a hardcore lifter? Does he squat a Mack truck, ass to the grass? Or is he doing lunges off a stability ball? This is when you know if he's got balls of steel and a cobra snake necktie or if he's into strength training (if you can call it strength training) for "metrosexual" reasons (not that there is anything wrong with that).

So the question for you is: do you want to *be* strong and powerful or do you want you quads to *look* long, sleek and toned? Well, guess what? You can have both! It comes at the high price of muscle soreness, but hey, you were willing to pay that price anyway when you got that gym membership, right?

Choosing the Right Exercises

When most guys lift for quad size and/or tone, they usually pick these four exercises: back squats, leg presses, lunges and leg extensions. Yet while these exercises can produce size and tone in the thighs overall, the size and tone produced by these exercises (with the exception of leg extensions) is not in the quadriceps. Sure, you'll get a big butt and some sore hamstrings if you squatted all the way down, but the front of your thighs, the quadriceps, will remain under stimulated and underdeveloped.

Why concentrate on developing your quadriceps? Look at an anatomy chart, and you'll find that the lines separating your quadriceps muscles are vertical. If you create muscle separation between the quadriceps muscles and if you develop the vastus medialis in particular (the tear drop quad muscle above your knees), then those vertical lines will make your thighs look powerful, yet long and sleek.

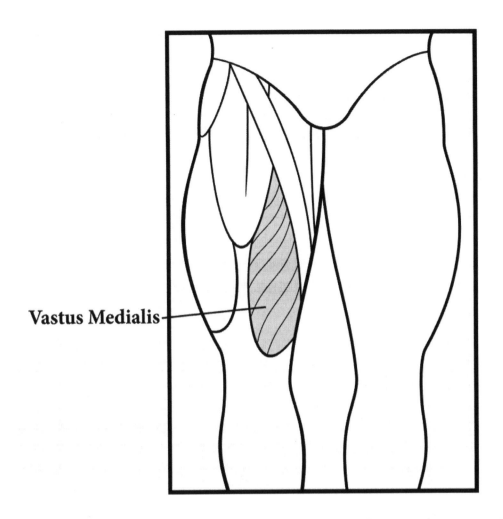

Vastus Medialis

Back squats, leg presses and lunges stress the quads somewhat, but they primarily stress the glutes, hips, inner thighs and hamstrings. Bodybuilders desire hamstring size, and I go into that in another chapter. Yet the development of the glutes, hips, and inner thighs will widen your thighs and make you look short and stocky. If you want the long, toned but powerful look for your quads, then you'll have to rethink your exercises:

Squat Variations

Most people don't even squat in the first place, and when they do they only squat till their thighs are parallel. Yet if you want big powerful thighs and a big powerful physique in general, then you need to do full range squats (any squats), PERIOD.

But for quad emphasis, which squat variation do you choose? Front squats or back squats?

The thing with back squats is that it will hit your hamstrings, hips and glutes a lot harder than your quadriceps. Don't believe me? Do a couple of heavy sets of full range 20 rep breathing back squats and tell me the next day where you feel sore.

That's right: you've got sore hamstrings and a sore ass (insert homo-erotic joke here). What about your quads? Any soreness? Unless that was your first time doing squats, then your answer would be a big, "NO!"

The **front squat**, however, hits your quadriceps much harder than back squats. When you do back squats, the bar is on you back, so you have to lean forward at the bottom to support and push the weight back up. This leaning forward activates the glutes and leaves your quads out of the action.

The front squat does the exact opposite. Since the bar is in front of your body, you have to support the weight in an upright position. You so much as lean forward, you'll lose control of the barbell and you've got crushed knees. Squatting in this upright position will activate your quads and your abdominals, leaving your glutes out of the picture. Hence you build up the long vertical lines of the quadriceps just above your knees instead of building up a big ass.

People who dare to squat usually back squat, because they can lift more weight and the exercise is not as technically demanding. The front squat, however, is more physically and mentally demanding, but far more rewarding for your physique. It is a man maker, because you must lift the weight with your whole entire body, not just your legs.

Another squat variation that's a quad builder is the **Hack squat**. Although the machine variation is OK, the barbell Hack squat stresses not only the vastus medialis, but like the front squat, it stresses the whole entire body. It is like performing a deadlift, but with the bar behind your back.

Sissy squats are another variation that stresses the vastus medialis muscle and minimizes glute development. It is a deceptively simple exercise to perform, but it will reveal to you just how strong you are at the knees. Most people find it difficult to perform just with bodyweight. If you're a badass and can perform more than 15 reps in strict form, then hold a 25 to 45 pound plate in your free hand for added resistance.

Lunge Variations

Forward lunges primarily stress the inner thighs and glutes. Some experts say you can shorten the stride of the lunge and that will develop the quads, but even then I have never found it to be an effective quad builder.

There is a lunge that builds the quads and that is the **reverse lunge**. All lunges regardless of stride length stress the glutes, and the reverse lunge is no exception. Yet unlike the forward lunge, the reverse lunge also hits the outer quads (the vastus lateralis and rectus femoris) hard. In fact, the reverse lunge will hit the outer quads harder than front squats, Hack squats, sissy squats or leg extensions, all of which primarily hit the vastus medialis.

So there you have it: the weapons and tools you can use in your quest for quad size.

IV. Steel-Cabled Hamstrings: Uncharted Territory for Size and Strength

For beginning to intermediate bodybuilders, the hamstrings remain the "undiscovered country" of size and strength. Most bodybuilders have a natural tendency to seek out and explore various exercises and programs for their upper bodies and even for their thighs in general. They end up discovering that squats and deadlifts add size not only to the thighs, but to the upper body as well.

Yet when it comes to program design specifically for the hamstrings, most bodybuilders (even veterans) are clueless. What happens is that bodybuilders will take the lessons they learned for quad size (20 rep breathing squats) and then apply these lessons inappropriately in their quests for hamstring size (ultra-high rep leg curls).

Twenty rep breathing squats will blow up your thighs till you look like a frog, and leg curls are essential to a thigh-building program, but high rep leg curls are useless. Yet most bodybuilders rely on high rep leg curls as their sole hamstring builder. You end up getting a bunch of bodybuilders with half built thighs: swollen quads, flat hamstrings.

So how do you build thick hamstrings that look like steel cables going down the back of your thighs? As always the answer lies in understanding 1) their fiber makeup and 2) appropriate exercise selection.

Strength, Speed, and Size!

The hamstrings consist of three muscles: the biceps femoris (which is all fast-twitch muscle fiber), the semitendinosus and the semimembranosus (both of which have a mix of fast and slow-twitch muscle fibers).

Although they have a mix of fast and slow-twitch fibers, over time and through consistent heavy training the semitendinosus and semimembranosus will respond more favorably to lower reps and heavier weight, just like their biceps femoris counterpart.

Since the hamstrings are composed primarily of fast-twitch muscle fiber, they are designed for power. What this means to you as a bodybuilder is that if you train your hamstrings for power then they will gain size as well. Muscular power is a combination of speed and strength. Now how do you train your hamstrings for power and size?

#1: **Go heavy!** The hamstrings respond extremely well to heavy weight at lower reps. Three to six reps is all you need. Anything more is just a waste of time.

#2: **Go heavy, but FAST!** What's power again?

Strength (heavy) + Speed (FAST!) = Power

Powerful hamstrings = BIG hamstrings

So it's important to choose a weight that is heavy, but is light enough to allow you to move the weight as fast as possible. Again, 3-6 reps is the norm.

#3: **Go heavy (but fast) over and over and over again!** Because you're using low reps, you have to make up for the lack of volume by doing multiple sets. Not 3-5 sets. Six and beyond. Without the added volume, you will not get the added size.

Exercise Selection for the Hamstrings

Hamstring exercises can be categorized into 2 parts: 1) exercises for the biceps femoris and 2) exercises for the semitendinosus and the semimembranosus. Perform an exercise from each category, and you will obtain complete hamstring development.

Exercises for the biceps femoris consist primarily of leg curl machines: standing, sitting and lying. This is the one occasion when you are required to use machines in order to develop a muscle. There is no free weight exercise that can activate the biceps femoris quite like the leg curl machines.

Yet why do people fail to build massive hamstrings on leg curls? The reason, again, is that they employ high reps (8-15). They think that because the leg curl is an isolation exercise, they should use high reps.

If you are looking to build thick hamstrings, then you as a bodybuilder need to get out of the "high rep/isolation exercise" mindset and employ multiple sets of low reps for leg curls. Instead of 3-4 sets of 12-15 reps for leg curls, try 8-10 sets of 3-5 reps.

Now for the semitendinosus and semimembranosus, you'll choose exercises that are variations of stiff-legged deadlifts. These include Romanian deadlifts and good mornings. Since the semitendinosus and semimembranosus have a mix of fast and slow-twitch muscle fibers, you can employ higher reps for these exercises.

The more months and years you train, however, the more your body will respond to lower reps and heavier weights. So while you may start out with 3 sets of10-12 reps on good mornings in your early phases of hamstring training, over time you'll be doing be 4 or more sets of 6-8 reps. As a bodybuilder, you will instinctively move towards lower reps, because you will find your hamstrings will respond better in size.

Remember the Mantra...

Go heavy. Go FAST! Over and over and over again. Do this, and your hamstrings will transform into bundles of steel cables.

V. Wingspan Workouts

I've always loved flexing my lats. Sure, other muscles are fun to pump up too, but no other pumped-up muscle can make you look instantly bigger than a pumped-up back. Gym rats who don't know any better constantly focus on the chest and the bench press for upper body size and strength. But a thick, wide, and strong back is the definition of brawn.

To help widen your latissimus dorsi, I'll provide you with 4 of the best shock techniques that I know to develop back width. These techniques are insanely difficult and painful, but you will reap tremendous size from them

Now, whether or not you have the guts to employ these techniques, you should always practice flexing your lats in and out of the gym. Most beginning bodybuilders don't know how to contract their back muscles. If you can't flex and harden your lats, then your nervous system is not activating enough fibers in your back to induce growth in that area. So practice your bodybuilding contest poses.

Now, without further ado...

"Shock Techniques to Widen Your Back"

Trisets

I'm a huge advocate for incorporating trisets into a hypertrophy program. Here is one triset that I use for back blasting:

1. **Pull-ups** (as many reps as you can do) followed immediately by
2. **Dumbbell pullovers** (8-10 reps) followed immediately by
3. **Stiff-arm pulldowns** (10-12 reps)

Rest 3-4 minutes
Repeat 2 more times

Make sure you get a good stretch on the pullovers and flex that those lats real hard on the stiff-arm pulldowns. If you're working out at home, and you don't have a cable machine, then you can substitute barbell rows for the stiff-arm pulldowns. For these barbell rows, however, you should use an underhand grip on an EZ-curl bar.

If you've never felt your lats fully flexed, then you will definitely feel it after the above triset. Only advanced bodybuilders should perform this technique. DO NOT even think about attempting this triset until you've learned how to perform the exercises properly by themselves.

10 sets of Pull-ups

Performing 10 sets of *any* exercise is going to induce growth. Before you attempt 10 sets of pull-ups, however, first figure out how many overhand pull-ups you can perform to failure. Divide that number by half: this is the number of reps you should perform for each of the ten sets. So if you can complete only 8 pull-ups, then you should attempt 10 sets of 4 reps. Rest one minute in between sets.

Note: you should know the number of pull-ups you can complete to failure *before* the day of the 10 set pull-up workout. Don't do a set of pull-ups to failure at the beginning of the workout to find out.

As you're working your way through the ten sets of pull-ups, you'll be tempted to perform more reps than you should. If you do, then you'll pay for it with less than spectacular growth. Every so often, however, figure out the number of pull-ups you can complete to failure and adjust your reps accordingly.

Chin-up/Pull-up Giant Set

You should notice by now that I recommend a lot of pull-ups for back width. Here's a giant set of pull-up variations that will blast every fiber in your back:

Wide-grip pull-ups (overhand grip) to failure. Rest 10 seconds.
Medium-grip pull-ups (overhand grip) to failure. Rest 10 seconds.
Medium-grip chin-ups (underhand grip) to failure. Rest 10 seconds.
Narrow-grip chin-ups to failure.
Rest 3-4 minutes, then repeat the entire process 2 more times.

Negative Pull-ups

Here's a way to perform negatives on pull-ups without the help of a spotter: place an Olympic barbell on a squat rack just high enough for you to perform pull-ups with your knees bent. Perform as many pull-ups as you can. When you cannot complete anymore pull-ups, stand up and position your body back at the top of the pull-up movement. Fold your legs again and perform a negative rep. Try to complete 3 negative reps at the end of every set of pull-ups.

There you have it, some of the most brutal techniques you can use to spread your wings.

VI. Bench press: Bodybuilding Style or Powerlifting Style?

One of the questions that I always ask my clients is, "What are your training goals?"

I don't accept general answers like "I want to be big and strong" or "I want to lose weight." I ask my clients to be VERY specific in what they want.

For example, here's a very specific goal: "I want to look like a classical bodybuilder with a V-taper: broad shoulders, small waist, and muscle tone."

That's specific. If you have a specific goal, then you can establish a specific game plan (i.e. your workout). If you know what you want, then you don't have to waste your time and energy doing something that doesn't help you achieve your goal.

Let's use the bench press as an example. Many people think that lifting for size and lifting for strength are one and the same.

To a certain extent, this is true. You can lift heavy on the bench press and develop enormous pecs. You'll get a bad case of man-boobs (or as one client of mine termed it, "fat-boy titties") but hey, you got size and strength, right?

When it comes to the bench press, you have to ask yourself, "What's my goal? Why am I using this exercise? Do I want to look good? Do I want to be strong?"

So ask yourself: do you want to be a bodybuilder, or do you want to be a powerlifter? Bodybuilders develop muscle with strength as a by-product, while powerlifters develop strength with size as a by-product.

Bodybuilders don't care about strength. They only care about the way their muscles look. Powerlifters, on the other hand, don't care about the way they look. They only care about lifting the most weight.

That's why bodybuilders and powerlifters perform the bench press in very different ways. Bodybuilders perform a variation of the bench press called the Neck Press, also known as the Guillotine Press. It looks like the bench press, but with one important difference: you lower the bar as close to your clavicles as you possibly can.

When most lifters (powerlifters and others) perform the bench press, they tend to lower the bar down on their nipples. While this may be the best way to lift the most weight, the Guillotine press is a far superior mass-builder than the conventional bench press.

By simply lowering the bar closer to your clavicles and keeping your elbows as far from your torso as possible, you give your pectorals a greater stretch, which induces greater muscle growth. This variation also induces more growth in the upper pecs and helps you avoid the man-boobs.

Two conditions before you attempt this variation:

1. When performing the Guillotine press, you should use less weight than you would normally use on the conventional bench press. Experiment first with lighter weight and add more weight when you feel comfortable.
2. Don't perform this movement if you have shoulder problems.

How do powerlifters perform the bench press? Powerlifters want to safely lift the most weight by any means necessary. That means getting the whole body into the movement, not just the chest. It also means shortening the distance in which you push.

They have a whole checklist of proper body mechanics for the lift from start to finish:

- Your feet should dig into the floor and your hamstrings should be flexed at a 45° angle.
- Grip the bar as hard as you can with a straight wrist "boxer's grip."
- Use a wide grip to shorten the distance of the lift.
- Squeeze your shoulder blades as hard you can as you bring the bar down.
- Lower to your nipple line to shorten the distance of the lift.
- Flex your "lats" as hard as you can and press the bar up.
- Don't just think of pressing the weight. Think of pushing yourself away from the bar and pushing your body into the bench.
- Press the bar off at a slight angle (away from the head and towards your waist) to shorten the distance of the lift.

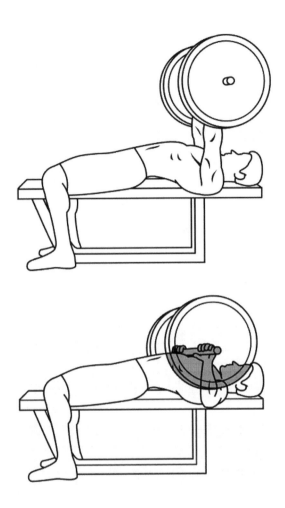

Think you got all that? Most people have a hard time implementing just one of these pointers. That's why it's a good idea to hire a qualified personal trainer to help you with the fine points of a lift, whether it's the Guillotine Press or the Powerlifter's Bench Press.

VII. Forging Those Armour Plates

The chest is, arguably, the bodypart most loved by bodybuilders. No other bodypart, aside from the arms, are paid quite as much attention to in the gym. Here are the best exercises for the chest that I've come across in all my years of training. This isn't the usual "bench press, incline press, dumbbell press, dumbbell flye" list for the chest, so pay attention to the directions outlined in this feature:

1) Gironda dips

This version of the dip is named after Vince Gironda, the Iron Guru who first came up with the idea to perform dips in this manner. It is the single best for the lower pectorals, hands downs! It's an excruciatingly difficult exercise to perform at first, but no other chest exercise is going to give you such immediate results.

To perform this exercise, you need a V-bar dipping station. Instead of gripping the bars with your palms facing each other (the way you would in regular dips), place your hands on the bars so that your palms facing away from each other. In this position, your elbows will stick out to the sides, which is what they should be doing throughout the exercise. With your fingers and thumbs on the inside of these bars, perform the dips with your body shaped liked a crescent moon. In other words round out your back (don't arch it!), keep your chest in a concave position, and keep your feet forward in front of you. Be sure you dip all the way down to really stretch those pecs.

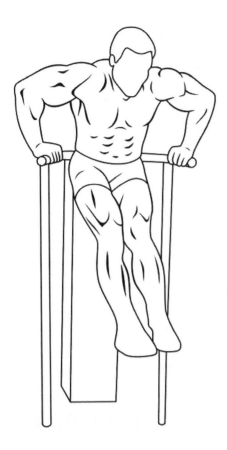

After just a few sets of this exercise, you'll wonder why your lower pecs never got this pumped before. There are a couple of caveats, however:

- If you have or had problems with shoulder pain, then don't perform this exercise.
- Perform Gironda dips at the end of your chest workout. This way your chest is thoroughly warmed up before you stretch it with this exercise.
- You're going to feel incredibly sore for a few days, but you'll definitely notice a thickness to your lower chest that wasn't there before.

2) Bench Press/Pushup compound set

Bodybuilders don't normally think of pushups as a mass builder for the chest. We usually of the bench press as the cornerstone exercise for pec size. Pushups as a set extender, however, will bring added mass and density to those pecs.

Here's what you do: perform any pressing movement for the chest. It could be the bench press, dumbbell incline press, or any other pressing movement. After you've gone to failure on that exercise and racked the bar (or dropped the dumbbells), immediately perform as many pushups as you can. You should perform these pushups while gripping a pair of dumbbells on the floor. The dumbbells should be positioned wide enough to give you the same grip as on the bench press. Make sure you descend all the way down on the pushup. If you want to stress the upper pecs more on the pushups, then perform them with your feet up on the bench.

A few of these compound sets and you'll stroll around the gym looking like an armored tank!

3) the Neck Press (a.k.a. the Guillotine Press)

It looks like the bench press, but with one important difference: you lower the bar as close to your clavicles as you possibly can. When most weightlifters perform the bench press, they tend to lower the bar down on their nipples. While this may be the best way to lift the most weight on the bench press, the Guillotine press is a far superior mass-builder than the conventional bench press. By simply lowering the bar to your neck and clavicle area and keeping your elbows as far from your torso as possible, you give your pectorals a greater stretch, which induces greater muscle growth.

Like Gironda dips, however, there are couple things you should note:

1. When performing the Guillotine press, you should use less weight than you would normally use on the conventional bench press. Experiment first with lighter weight, then add more weight when you feel comfortable.
2. Don't perform this movement if you have shoulder problems.

4) the 20º press

This movement should be self-explanatory. By performing dumbbell presses or barbell presses on a 20-30º incline, you'll target the upper pecs. The problem, however, is that most incline benches are far too steep (they're usually at 45º). Performing incline presses at such a steep angle will stress more of your frontal deltoids and very little of your upper pecs. In fact, MRI studies show that decline presses will hit your upper pecs just as much as the 45º incline press.

If your gym doesn't have any 20-30° incline benches, then don't worry about it. If you want to emphasize your upper pecs on a 45° incline bench, then use a narrower grip (about shoulder width). Guillotine presses and pushups with your feet elevated will also hit your upper pecs.

5) Dumbbell Presses

Mature bodybuilders seem to instinctively know that for virtually all upper body exercises involving free weights, dumbbell movements are superior to their barbell counterparts in stimulating mass. For example, dumbbell bench presses pack more meat on your pecs than barbell bench presses.

The reason dumbbell movements tend to be superior to barbell movements has to do with neuromuscular stimulation. The greater the balance and coordination needed to move a weight, the greater the neuromuscular stimulation. When you lift dumbbells, more muscle fibers are recruited to perform the movement. Greater fiber recruitment translates to greater growth.

6) Machine Flyes

I may be in the minority, but when it comes to stretch-induced growth in the pectorals, I think machine flyes are superior to dumbbell flyes (provided that you're using the right machine). If you're using one of those padded pec deck machines where you're performing a shoulder adduction with the arms externally rotated (in other words, each of your arms is L-shaped as if you're in the middle of performing a military press), then you could incur long term damage to your shoulder joints.

Instead, use a pec deck with a pair of handles for you to grip rather than a couple of pads. Such an exercise on this type of machine more closely resembles the movement of dumbbell flyes, which is much safer.

I like performing machine flyes instead of dumbbell flyes for a couple of reasons. With dumbbell flyes, all you feel is a stretch at the bottom third of the movement. But with machine flyes, there's constant tension on your pecs all throughout the motion of the exercise. Thus, not only do you get a good stretch at the beginning of each concentric rep, but you also fully contract your chest at the end of each concentric rep (unlike dumbbell flyes or the bench press).

The other reason that machine flyes are better than dumbbell flyes is that negatives are much more effective on a pec deck. Give this a try: after several sets on the bench press, finish off your chest workout with a few sets of machine flyes. For each set on the pec deck, select a weight that will allow you to perform 10-12 reps in a quick tempo fashion.

After you go to failure somewhere between the 10th and 12th rep, immediately perform 3 negatives with the next highest weight. Make sure that with each rep, you fight the force of the weight until you're stretching back as far as you can go. Have a partner assist you in bringing the handles of the machine back to the beginning of each negative rep.

You shouldn't perform these eccentric sets all the time; just once every 2 weeks. Periodically performing negatives on the deck, however, will definitely provide you with consistent gains in chest size.

As you can see from this list, stretching, tension, and angle of execution are the three most important factors in training for chest size. Regardless of your choice of exercises, make sure you incorporate these factors in your chest program.

VIII. Direct Assault: The "Case" for Arm Training

Recently there's been a trend of abbreviated training routines. In these routines, basic compound movements such as the bench press and barbell rows are emphasized, but direct arm work is nonexistent.

The argument that's asserted for such routines is that direct arm work does very little to incur hypertrophy. Supposedly, the hypertrophy derived from direct arm work is negligible at best.

Well, I'm here to tell you that if you want bigger arms, you need to train them directly. I bet you're saying, "Duh, Einstein. I never stopped training my arms."

Yes, yes, most trainees are reluctant to give up their concentration curls and cable pressdowns, but who's ever gotten big arms off of concentration curls and cable pressdowns alone? And don't think you're getting bigger arms from dips, barbell curls and close grip bench presses either. Compound exercises alone will not help you achieve bigger and more muscular-looking arms.

There are a number of reasons why many trainees do not achieve massive arms through direct training, but three factors stand out:

1) Inappropriate exercise selection
2) Inappropriate set totals
3) Inappropriate repetition protocols

Inversely, there are number of reasons why some trainees maintain or even temporarily increase their arm size on abbreviated programs. For one thing, since most trainees never properly train their arms, not much growth is gained. So when these trainees employ an abbreviated program, they don't lose much arm mass at all. How can you lose what you never even gained in the first place?

Now some trainees may increase their arm size on abbreviated programs, but this is due to a sudden drop in training volume. Much of the increase in arm size is due to water weight. This sarcoplasmic hypertrophy is due to the accumulation of muscle glycogen resulting from a lack of direct training. Sarcoplasmic hypertrophy is temporary and only lasts for a few days.

To properly train your arms, you need to understand the fiber composition of your upper arm muscles:

FAST-TWITCH, FAST-TWITCH, FAST-TWITCH!

Yes, your arms have a high amount of fast-twitch muscle fibers. So it makes sense that if you want to maximize the size of your arms, you must stress the fibers with the greatest growth potential.

Question is: where are these fast-twitch fibers?

Target #1: The Brachialis

While your biceps have a mix of fast and slow-twitch fibers, the misnamed "lower biceps" or brachialis is composed primarily of fast-twitch fibers. Even though it is only the size of a golf ball, the brachialis is situated underneath your biceps next to the inside of your elbow. With regards to symmetry, this is a strategic location on your arm. Develop the brachialis, and its increased size will push the biceps up and give you greater biceps "peak." Greater biceps peak adds to greater arm girth.

Exercises that target the brachialis include hammer curls (incline and standing), preacher curl variations, reverse grip EZ-bar curls, and Zottman curls.

To perform Zottman curls, simply take a pair of dumbbells in either a standing or seated position and curl them up. Once you've curled them to the top position, rotate your wrists so that your hands are pronated and your palms are facing the floor. From this position, lower the dumbbells slowly. Once you reach the bottom, repeat this method of curling and lowering for the desired number of reps. The Zottman curl is an excellent movement that works the brachialis, bicep, and forearm.

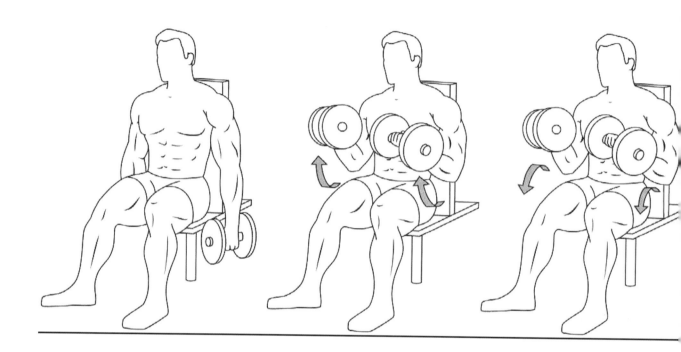

Target #2: The Triceps Long Head

Of the three triceps heads (lateral, medial, and long head), the long head of the triceps is the meatiest of the three. Even when the lateral and medial heads are fully developed and the long head is underdeveloped, the long head is still comparable in size.

Whereas the lateral and medial heads have a mix of fast and slow-twitch fibers, the long head is comprised primarily of fast-twitch fibers. So when the fibers of the triceps long head are properly stressed, they develop tremendous size.

Now while the bench press, close grip bench press and dips are excellent mass builders for the lateral and medial triceps heads, the long head is almost inactive during these exercises. This is one reason why abbreviated programs can never fully develop the upper arms.

Exercises targeting the long head are 1) lying flat bench triceps extensions with an EZ curl bar and 2) lying decline extensions with an EZ curl bar. If you perform either one of these extension movements in conjunction with a pressing movement, then you will develop thick, full triceps. Performing lying triceps extensions with a straight barbell or dumbbells, however, will shift the emphasis to the lateral heads.

Set and Rep Protocols for the Upper Arms

You know where the fast-twitch fibers are on your arms, and you know what exercises isolate these fibers. Question is: what sort of set and rep protocol should you use?

Everyone who's familiar with fiber type training knows that fast-twitch muscle fibers require heavy weight and low reps. What a lot of trainees fail to do, however, is employ multiple sets of these low reps. Two to three sets of 4-6 reps just doesn't incur much growth, but the next ten sets of 4-6 reps sure does the trick.

A Sample Program

The following is a sample program to stimulate the fast-twitch fibers of your upper arms. On Monday you'll perform supersets with a minute and a half between the two exercises listed. On Wednesday you'll perform high reps with no rest between the exercises and a minute rest between supersets. These high reps will help promote recovery between the fast twitch training sessions. On Friday, you'll perform ten consecutive sets of biceps, followed by ten consecutive sets of triceps.

Monday

A1) Preacher curls (6 sets) 6 reps, 90 seconds rest
  - You can use any variation of the preacher curl. Variations include the straight barbell preacher curl, one arm dumbbell preacher curls or reverse grip EZ-bar preacher curls

A2) Lying flat bench triceps extensions with an EZ curl bar (6 sets) 6 reps, 90 seconds rest

Wednesday

A1) Lying to seated dumbbell curls (3 sets) 13-15 reps, no rest
  - Perform 6-8 reps of lying flat bench dumbbell curls, then sit up and perform alternating seated dumbbell curls

A2) Elevated diamond pushups (3 sets) 13-15 reps, 60 seconds rest
  - Place your hands on the floor and form a diamond shape
  - Place your feet on a bench
  - Perform as many pushups as you can, aiming for 13-15 reps

Friday

A) Incline hammer curls (10 sets) 4 reps, 60 seconds rest

B) Seated overhead half press in power rack (10 sets) 4 reps, 60 seconds rest
  - Sit upright on a bench inside a power rack
  - Set the pins of the rack at forehead level and place the barbell on top of them
  - Grasp the barbell with a shoulder width grip, no wider
  - Press the barbell from the pins to lockout

To launch a direct assault on your arms, you need to lift the heavy artillery. Bottom line: big arms need big weight and must be trained directly.

IX. Branding a Pair of Horseshoes

The triceps are a muscle that's misunderstood by many bodybuilders. For example, in every gym there are beginners who just do pressdowns. Then there's the guy who wants some mass in his triceps, so he performs nothing but close grip bench presses and dips. Then there's the guy who performs lying triceps extensions to the forehead with the wrong tempo.

Listen, nobody ever got big triceps off of pressdowns alone. You're a fool to believe that close grip presses and dips are the keys to massive triceps. And any idiot who performs skull crushers with quick, brisk reps should add a 100 more pounds on that EZ-curl bar and let it crush his puny little brain of his!

Wheww! Sorry. As you can tell, I'm in the middle of my dieting phase. Seriously though, most bodybuilders don't know how to develop massive triceps to balance out their biceps. Even Arnold had to play catch-up with his triceps to balance out his incredibly peaked bi's.

"So, Mr. Know It All: what's the big secret to massive triceps?"

First, I don't know it all; nobody does. Anyone who says he does is trying to sell you something. Second, it's not a big secret, but a bunch of little secrets that make up triceps size. If you want to discover these secrets, however, you should understand the differences between the different triceps heads.

Long Head vs. Lateral and Medial

Do a biceps pose right now: If the long head of your triceps is well developed, then the bottom of your upper arm should be curving downward (provided that you're not fat, of course). Do you have an idea now, which one your triceps heads is not well developed?

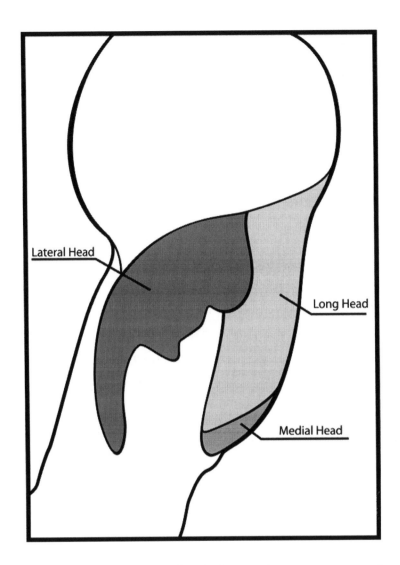

Most bodybuilders don't know how to properly develop the long head of their triceps, which is the meatiest portion. The laterals and medial heads are easily accessed whenever you perform any pressing movements, whether its bench presses, pressdowns, military presses, or dips.

The long head, however, is not activated very much by these exercises. I don't care what MRI or EMG studies say. None of the aforementioned exercises activate the long head, not even dips, which is a supposed mass builder.

This is why when you select triceps exercises, you should perform at least two exercises: one for the long head, one for the lateral and medial heads.

Anyone who performs only close grip presses or dips in the hopes of attaining thick, full triceps will be sorely disappointed.

How to Access the Long Head:

1. Choose the appropriate exercise
2. Complete the appropriate number of reps
3. Execute the appropriate tempo
4. Take the appropriate amount of rest in between sets

Choosing Exercises

When it comes to targeting the long head, any of the triceps extension exercises would be appropriate. Some, however, are better than others. I've never found overhead extensions, such as the French press or overhead dumbbell extensions, to be good mass builders. My favorites are the 45° French press and lying triceps extensions (a.k.a. skull crushers). I prefer to perform these exercises one arm at a time with a dumbbell. Although beginners should perform them with an EZ-curl bar, mature bodybuilders should work out with dumbbells and engage in unilateral (single arm) training every so often.

To perform the 45° French press, grab an EZ-curl barbell or a dumbbell and sit back on a 45° incline bench. Elevate your body high enough so that you can extend the weight above your face and lower it behind your head with your elbows back as far as possible.

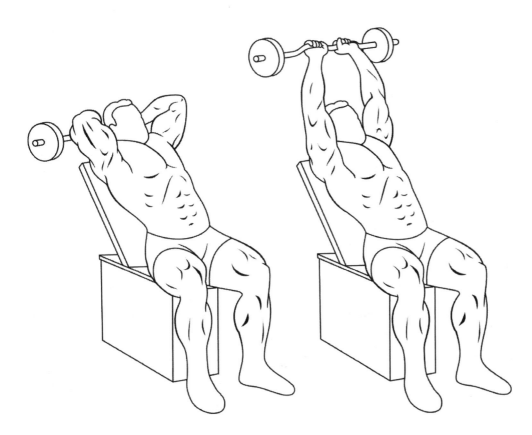

To perform a rep, fully extend the weight directly over your head, allowing your elbows to move forward slightly, but keeping your upper arms close to your face. Reverse the movement and stretch the triceps as far back as possible.

If you're using a dumbbell or two, start the movement off with a semi-supinated grip. When approaching the top of the movement, rotate the dumbbells till your grip is pronated. Flex hard at the top.

As for flat bench lying triceps extensions, perform the same rotation with the dumbbells. When you lower the weight (barbell or dumbbell), however, don't lower it till it touches your forehead. Lower the weight until it touches a spot on the bench above the top of your head. This allows for a greater stretch than "skull-crushers".

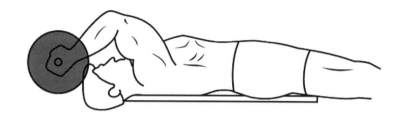

Allow your elbows to move back slightly, keeping your upper arms close to your face. As soon you touch the bench, fully extend the weight directly over you. Make sure that when you lie on the bench, you have enough of a bench above your head for you to touch. If you don't, then you'll lower the weight over the end of the bench, which would resemble a pullover more than an extension.

Rep Range

The long head of the triceps responds only to high loads, because it's composed mostly of fast-twitch muscle fibers. Whereas the lateral and medial heads respond to a wide variety of reps, low to moderate reps for the long head would be appropriate. You'll have to experiment to find the appropriate rep protocols for you, but I find that a continuum of 4-8 reps with a 4-6 target rep range right for most bodybuilders.

Rest Periods

Because of its high fast-twitch makeup, working the long head requires long rest periods. Three to four minutes between sets should be enough.

Tempo

Almost all exercises for the long head require that you slow it down in order to feel any sort of tension from the movement. When performing 45° French presses or lying extensions, always slow down the eccentric portion of the movement. You can always vary the speed of the eccentric, just make sure the speeds are slow enough that you can feel the weight.

As for the concentric portion of these movements, you can also vary the speed. Unlike the eccentric portion, however, you can perform the concentric portion at high speeds if you're using heavy weight. To reiterate:

Eccentric: somewhat slow to super slow
Concentric: somewhat slow to explosive

One last note on triceps training: always perform isotension on triceps. In other words, flex them in between sets and when you're not working out. This will help you exercise better muscle control, which translates to greater fiber recruitment when you hit the weights. Follow this game plan, and you'll have a pair of those lucky horseshoes in no time.

X. Biceps: The Pinnacle of Brawn

Quick! Make a muscle!

What did you do? You flexed your biceps, of course. Ever since Popeye, the bicep has been the symbol of strength and brawn. Yet the great thing about biceps training is that it fun to do. There is something very satisfying about feeling and watching your arms bulge as you pump them up. It is almost as if you get a sense of immediate gratification when training biceps.

Nevertheless, it's important to put a little planning into your biceps training. Here are some of the strategies you can employ to get bulging biceps:

<u>Angles, angles, angles!</u>

The biceps is very sensitive to different angles of movement. Performing incline curls will give you quite a different feel in the biceps as opposed to preacher curls. Because of this angle sensitivity, the biceps love a variety of exercises.

For complete hypertrophy, you'll need to concern yourself with 4 types of angles for the biceps:

Curling the weight with the elbows behind you (i.e. lying dumbbell curls)
Curling the weight with the elbows in front of you (i.e. concentration curls)
Curling the weight with the elbows beside you (i.e. Zottman curls)
Curling the weight with the elbows above you (i.e. behind the neck cable curls)

There are exceptions to the above categories, and such biceps movements involve moving your elbows from angle to angle (i.e. perfect curls). Of all of the angles, the most important one for hypertrophy is #1: curling the weight with weight with the elbows behind you.

The reason is that you are performing the lift in a stretched position. The greater the stretch on the biceps: the greater the tension on the muscle. After all, you lift weights to create muscular tension. The greater the muscular tension: the greater the hypertrophy.

Therefore, if you were pressed for time and were restricted to one biceps movement, then choose a curl in the stretched position, such as incline hammer curls.

Priming the Pump: Compound Sets, Trisets and Other Set Extenders

Bodybuilders love training the biceps, since the muscle responds so well to the pump. This is why trisets, compound sets, and giant sets work so well on the biceps.

Here's a triset that I use to pump up the biceps from time to time:

Incline dumbbell curls
Standing dumbbell curls
Behind the neck cable curls

Dumbbells vs. Barbells

Biceps respond much better to dumbbell curls as opposed to barbell curls. The reason is you can change the grip from movement to movement and within the movement itself. Changing the grip will activate different portions of the biceps. While performing curls palms up will activate the two heads of the biceps, performing curls with the hands in a neutral position or palms down position will activate the brachialis. This leads to the next biceps tip:

Target the Brachialis

While your biceps have a mix of fast and slow-twitch fibers, the misnamed "lower biceps" or brachialis is composed primarily of fast-twitch fibers. Even though it is only the size of a golf ball, the brachialis is situated underneath your biceps next to the inside of your elbow. With regards to symmetry, this is a strategic location on your arm. Develop the brachialis, and its increased size will push the biceps up and give you greater biceps "peak." Greater biceps peak adds to greater arm girth.

Biceps training consists of a lot of fun movements, full of variety and immediate gratification. So head out to gym and mix it up!

XI. Cattle Call

Calves: there is no other body part in which genetics plays such an enormous role. Bodybuilders throughout the years have experimented with numerous methods to induce growth in the calves, from jump-roping to wearing crazy shoes to ultra-high reps. Not one, however, has come up with a routine or technique that consistently produces results for the average person.

Until now...

O.K., maybe I'm being a little overly dramatic, but quite frankly, this technique that I'm going to reveal to you is the best method (that I've developed) for inducing growth in the calves. I have never come across a technique that even comes close to this one. If you employ this technique intermittently (every third workout, at most), then you will see some definite improvements in your calf size.

I must emphasize this, however: you can use this method only if you're an advanced bodybuilder who's been religiously training his or her calves for a few years. If you've never trained your calves before or have not pushed yourself to the limit in calf training, then explore various other calf training methods before employing this technique.

O.K., having said that little disclaimer, here's how it works:

You will need a dumbbell rack, a calf block, and something stable to hold on to (like an incline bench or a machine). The exercise you will be performing is what I call "dumbbell calf raises." I can't remember from whom I picked this exercise up from first: Dan Duchaine or Steve Holman. Regardless of who invented it or who discovered it, the dumbbell calf raise is the best calf exercise (yes, even better than donkey calf raises).

For those of you who don't know how to perform this exercise, take a dumbbell of an appropriate weight (say, 20 pounds) in one hand and with the other hand, hold on to a heavy, stable piece of equipment. Place the foot from the same side as the weight onto the edge of a calf block. With that foot, and that foot alone, perform some calf raises.

If your calf block is padded, then I suggest you perform the raises without any shoes. This will allow for greater range of motion, which means a deeper stretch and greater contraction for your calves.

To illustrate, if you're performing calf raises with your left foot first, then you would be holding the dumbbell at your side with your left hand. Your right hand would be holding on to something to maintain your balance. Your right foot wouldn't be touching anything at all.

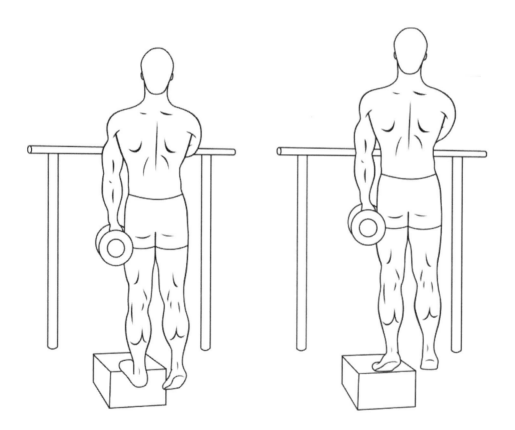

There are two reasons why this exercise is so effective. First, the weight with which your calf is lifting (your body plus the dumbbell) is unstable. Unless you're a ballerina, most people would find it difficult tiptoeing a dozen times on the edge of a block. If you're new to the exercise, then performing it with your bodyweight alone will be difficult. The instability of the dumbbell calf raise makes it superior to the traditional standing machine calf raise, where the weight is stabilized.

The other reason for this exercise's effectiveness is that you're training one limb at a time, which is known as unilateral training. When one limb is forced to handle a weight by itself, your nervous system recruits more fibers in that muscle. If you've never performed the dumbbell calf raise, then I suggest you train your calves with this exercise until you're no longer making any progress with it before moving on to the technique below.

O.K., now that you know how to perform the exercise, let's incorporate the shock technique known as "descending sets," otherwise known as "strip sets" or "down the rack." After you've warmed up your calves, grab a weight that will allow you to crank out 8-10 reps to failure on the dumbbell calf raise.

For example, work the right calf in a steady and continuous tempo, then switch the weight from your right hand to your left hand and immediately work the left calf with the same tempo. That's one strip set.

Once you're finished, immediately grab a lighter dumbbell and crank out another 8-10 reps to failure on your right calf, then on your left calf. That's a second strip set. Repeat this process two more times, for a total of four strip sets. On your fifth and final strip set, perform one-legged calf raises without a dumbbell. Rest for 2-3 minutes, and repeat the entire process with slightly less weight.

Here's how it would look step by step:

Dumbbell Calf Raises (For each set, alternate between your left and right calf without resting unless indicated)
1st set: 10-12 reps w/ 25 lb. Dumbbell
2nd set: 10-12 reps w/ 20 lb. Dumbbell

3rd set: 10-12 reps w/ 15 lb. Dumbbell
4th set: 10-12 reps w/ 10 lb. Dumbbell
5th set: 10-12 reps w/ bodyweight only
Rest 2-3 minutes
6th set: 10-12 reps w/ 20 lb. Dumbbell
7th set: 10-12 reps w/ 15 lb. Dumbbell
8th set: 10-12 reps w/ 10 lb. Dumbbell
9th set: 10-12 reps w/ 5 lb. Dumbbell
10th set: 10-12 reps w/ bodyweight only
> perform all sets to failure
> use a full range of motion
> use a steady and continuous tempo

In performing the above technique, you would have completed a total of 20 sets (10 for each calf) in only 5-8 minutes, assuming that you didn't rest at all between strip sets. As you can see, it's a very intense technique. For this reason, I don't recommend employing this method all the time. Once a week is more than enough. For your other calf workouts, train them as you would normally train them.

Don't do this workout unless you really pushed yourself to the limit when training your calves in the past. Otherwise, your calves are going to be locked up in rigor mortis, and you'll be walking around on your tippy-toes. And don't even think about doing this workout less than a week before an athletic event... unless of course you're a ballerina.

XII. Carving Out Those Boulder Shoulders

Everybody wants Steve Reeves' shoulders. In all honesty, his deltoid development wasn't exceptionally impressive, but he was blessed with god-like shoulder width in his skeletal frame that made up for any flatness in his deltoid muscles.

For us mere mortals, however, we have to work our shoulders to obtain some kind of width. I, myself, have narrow shoulders, so I've always paid special attention to my lateral delts.

As you can probably guess, this article is about creating the illusion of width in your shoulders. We should, however, examine the differences between the 3 heads that comprise the deltoid muscle group.

The Lateral Head

This is the head that you want to focus on to create the illusion of width in the shoulders. You want to develop the bulbous look of this head, so that you have some separation between it and your biceps and triceps. If your lateral head became flat, not only would you lose the illusion of wide shoulders but your arms would also look fat if you had large biceps and triceps.

To develop the lateral head, you should use a wide variety of reps, but focus on the Type IIa and Type I fibers. In other words, you should complete a higher number of reps with little or no rest. This is why set extension techniques such trisets and descending sets work particularly well for the lateral head.

The Posterior Head

This is the least developed deltoid in bodybuilders. Although many bodybuilders perform bent-over lateral raises, this exercise is actually a poor choice for developing the posterior deltoid. With bent-over laterals, there is a tendency to cheat and swing the weights up with the help of the upper back muscles, the trapezius, and the legs.

To develop the rear deltoids, I prefer the exercise known as "lying reverse flyes." This is simply an exercise where you lie on your side and perform the rear delt raises one arm at a time. The lying reverse flye is a superior exercise, because it allows for a greater stretch of the posterior deltoid when the dumbbell passes across the chest and comes close to the floor.

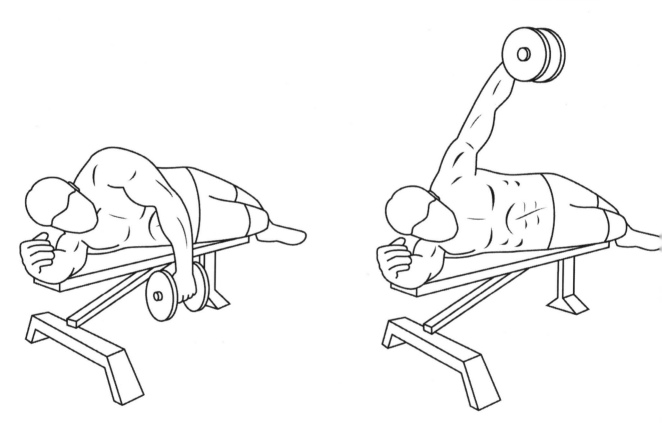

The Anterior Head

This is the head you need to worry about the least. Most bodybuilders perform plenty of bench presses, incline presses, and military presses to develop this deltoid. Even when it comes to standing lateral raises, the anterior head will activate if you use poor form (which most people do). Unless you're lacking in anterior head development, I would skip front delt training altogether. Since they're mostly made up of fast-twitch fibers, heavy pressing (from any angle) will activate the anterior heads.

<u>Techniques for Increasing Lateral Deltoid Size:</u>

Lean Away Laterals (Descending Sets)--In order to stimulate growth in my lateral delts, I developed this brutal method for my workouts. It's the best one I've come across. Here's what you do: Perform 3 sets of lean away dumbbell lateral raises. Each set is comprised of 4 descending sets. Rest 90 seconds between each arm.

Here's a sample workout:

Lean away dumbbell laterals (10-12 reps at 25 lbs.) Use left arm. Followed immediately by
(8-10 reps at 20 lbs.) followed immediately by
(6-8 reps at 15 lbs.) followed immediately by
(6-8 reps at 10 lbs.)
Rest for 90 seconds, then repeat the entire process for the right arm
Switch back and forth between the right and left arm for 2 more times

Shoulders Triset--This triset consists of 8-12 reps of standing dumbbell laterals, followed immediately by 8-12 reps of wide grip upright barbell rows, followed immediately by 8-12 reps of dumbbell overhead presses. Rest for 2 minutes, then repeat the entire process 2 more times.

I should warn you that performing too much work on the trapezius muscle (i.e. narrow grip upright rows) can make narrow shoulders look even narrower. My advice to bodybuilders with narrow frames is to abandon any direct trap work. People with narrow shoulders develop immense traps without even training them directly. For these folks, any standing upper body exercises work will develop their traps.

Bow and Press--Here's an exercise from the bodybuilding genius, the late Vince Gironda, a man way ahead of his time. This exercise places continuous tension on all three deltoid heads. Grab a pair of dumbbells that you would normally use for laterals. Hold them in front of you, as if you're about to complete a biceps curl, with the elbows slightly forward. From this position, move your arms out to the sides till it looks like you're forming a "W." At this point, press the dumbbells up in an arc, keeping your elbows as far back as possible.

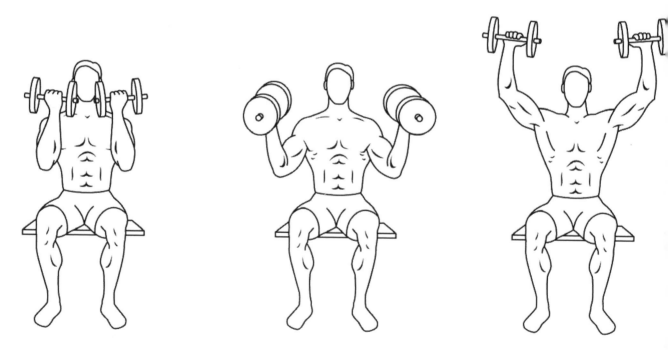

That's one rep. Now slowly reverse the movement and perform 8-12 reps. Make sure you perform this entire movement slowly. This will give you a burn in your shoulders that you've never felt before.

Overhead Dumbbell Press (Pinkies Up)--Here's how Arnold would tweak his overhead dumbbell presses: he would lift the dumbbells with his pinky side higher than his thumb side. This may not seem like a significant change in form, but if you incorporate this little trick, you'll hit the lateral deltoids much harder. Here are some other tips to remember:

- Perform this movement standing with a slight lean forward. If you perform dumbbell overhead press sitting in a chair with back support, then there'll be a tendency for you to lean back, which would shift the focus to your front delts
- Keep your elbows as far back as possible throughout the movement to keep the stress on the lateral delts
- Press the movement up in the form of an arc
- Go for lower to moderate reps on this movement (6-10 reps)
- You can also incorporate descending sets into this exercise as well:

Standing Overhead Dumbbell Presses (Pinkies Up, Elbows Back): 6-8 reps followed immediately by
8-10 reps with lighter weight followed immediately by
10-12 reps with lighter weight
Rest for 60-90 seconds
Repeat the entire process 2 more times

If you still can't get boulder shoulders after blasting away with these techniques, then you're out of luck. But hey, who knows? Maybe those shoulder pads from the 80's will be in fashion again.

XIII. Postural Realignment: The Key to Strength and Physique

Sometimes you pursue a goal and not realize you took a major detour into the proverbial wrong side of town. When you finally realize you're no longer in Kansas, you think to yourself, "What the hell happened? How the hell did I end up here?"

That "what the hell?" moment occurred to me when I was trying on a suit at the Men's Wearhouse. I looked in the three-way mirror and didn't see myself, but a Neanderthal. This throwback from the Ice Age had rounded shoulders, a forward head posture and overly pronated hands, which were holding a wooden club and a rock.

OK, so the Neanderthal standing in front of the three-way mirror at the Men's Wearhouse wasn't holding anything. And no, I did not de-evolve and turn into a Neanderthal. Nevertheless, at that moment I realized that I had horrible posture that was severely detracting from my physique.

"What the Hell Happened?"

What happened was that for years, I trained as a recreational bodybuilder hell bent on gaining size in the chest at all costs. Like a lot of bodybuilders, I wanted huge pecs like Arnold, doing a lot of bench presses, dumbbell presses and dips.

Unfortunately, just like *a lot of bodybuilders*, I didn't include enough sets and exercises for other body parts to balance out the high volume I was placing on the chest. I didn't include enough back work (such as seated cable rows) to counteract all of the pressing movements.

And to avoid overtraining my shoulders, I cut out overhead pressing movements, like the military press. A lot of "gurus" tell you to cut out direct shoulder work, since the deltoids get plenty of work from bench presses and back work.

Well guess what?   As an inexperienced lifter at the time, my misguided desire for thick pecs coupled with the bad advice of supposed training gurus turned me into "Og!" the caveman.

After I saw myself in the three-way mirror, I was no longer hell bent on building a massive chest (which I built to an impressive density and thickness) but on fixing my posture and regaining a more striking and august physique (think Greek warrior).

What is good posture? Think boot camp: chin up, eyes forward (not down), chest out, shoulders back, stomach in, head and neck in line with your spine, no slouching.

Fixing Your Posture Through Strength Training

Sometimes what you know gets you into trouble, and sometimes that same knowledge gets you out of trouble. I know weight training. Years of unbalanced weight training programs had taken its toll on my body and transformed me into Og!, but I knew that a properly balanced strength training program would help me regain a classical bodybuilding physique.

So what I ended doing was dropping chest exercises altogether.

That's right: no chest work. No bench presses, no incline presses, no dumbbell presses, no dumbbell flyes, no cable flyes, no pec deck. NOTHING.

Of course being the bodybuilding addict that I was, I weaned myself off chest work little by little, because I was irrationally fearful of my chest losing its thickness. But I had such a big chest (insert man-boob joke here), that I didn't lose much thickness, size or density at all when I detrained.

Aside from cutting out the chest exercises, I incorporated back, shoulder and neck exercises to bring my shoulders and neck back into alignment. The program I developed addressed these areas of postural realignment:

- Incorporate scapula retraction movements
- Incorporate neck extensions
- Incorporate overhead pressing
- Strengthen the rotator cuff
- Strengthen the posterior deltoid
- Strengthen the transverse abdominus
- Stretch the pectorals

Scapula Retraction

Bring your arms up and back. Squeeze your shoulder blades in as far they can go. You should feel the muscles in between your shoulder blades tense up.

That is a scapula retraction. Most people fail to add this tiny but important detail when they perform back exercises such as deadlifts or seated cable rows. In fact, if you perform back exercises without this tiny detail, then these incomplete back movements will worsen your posture.

Aside from deadlifts and cable rows, there are other back exercises specifically addressing scapula retraction. These movements include face pulls, cable neck rows and "the Cactus."

The Cactus is great, because you can perform it any place with a wall. All you have to do is place your back against the wall with your feet in front of you and your legs at an angle towards the wall. Bring your arms up as if you're being robbed at gunpoint.

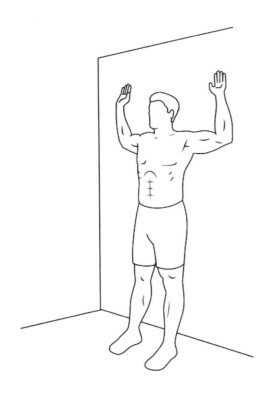

From this position, flatten every part of your upper body against the wall. Squeeze your shoulder blades in and stick your chest out. Bring your head, shoulders, elbows, and wrists back and press them all against the wall. Tighten you abs and bring them in, as there should be no gap in the small of your lower back. In fact, there should be no gaps anywhere between your upper body and the wall.

Hold this position for as long as you can and breathe shallow. Once you cannot hold it any longer, relax and take in a few deep breathes and repeat 2 to 4 more times.

Neck Extensions

Here is another exercise you can perform against the wall, called a "wall bridge." If you have a forward head posture, then this exercise will bring you head and neck back into alignment with your spine.

To perform the wall bridge, simply press the back of your head (just below the crown) against a wall. Your feet will be in front of you so that your body will be leaning against the wall at a 60° angle. Maintain a straight body posture, and keep your head and neck in line with your spine. Do not let your body sag, and press the back top of your head against the wall for as long as you can.

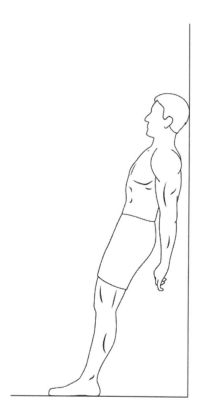

When you can no longer maintain the position, step away from the wall. If you've done it correctly, then your head and neck should pull back into alignment with your spine and you should immediately feel taller.

Overhead Pressing

Many people have difficulty performing overhead presses (such as the barbell military press) due to shoulder pain. One way around this is to perform overhead presses with dumbbells as opposed to a barbell. The disadvantage to any barbell overhead pressing is that the barbell locks your arms into a fixed angle when you lift, which can be stressful to your shoulder joints.

With dumbbell overhead pressing, however, you can adjust your arm positioning as you lift the weight. So rather than having your arms extend out at an angle as you press the weight up, you can press the weight up by extending your arms straight up and down in alignment with your body. This type of pressing is much gentler on your shoulder joints.

Not only that, but dumbbells allow you to start off with your hands in a neutral position instead of a pronated position. A neutral hand positioning is more natural and is less stressful on your joints than the pronated hand positioning used in barbell military pressing.

Now whether or not you use dumbbells or barbells for overhead pressing, always press the weight up in alignment with your body. Many people press the weight up at a slight angle in front of their bodies. If you press the weight up and you can see your arms through your peripheral vision, then you know you've got poor alignment.

To remedy this, bring your arms back, squeeze your shoulder blades, and tighten your abs throughout the press. Your arms should be out of your peripheral vision as you lift.

Rotator Cuff Work

There are plenty of rotator cuff exercises from which to choose from. The bottom line is you'll need to do one or two of them to help stabilize your shoulder joint. What I recommend is to pyramid your weight up until you're comfortably in the 6-8 rep range. People always use high reps for the rotator cuff, but the fact of the matter is the rotator cuff is comprised mostly of tendons and fast-twitch muscle fiber. Hence, you'll get much better shoulder stabilization by using moderate weight and moderate reps.

The Posterior Deltoid

This is the least developed deltoid in bodybuilders. Although many bodybuilders perform bent-over lateral raises, this exercise is actually a poor choice for developing the posterior deltoid. With bent-over laterals, there is a tendency to cheat and swing the weights up with the help of the upper back muscles, the trapezius, and the legs.

To develop the rear deltoids, I prefer the exercise known as "lying reverse flyes." This is simply an exercise where you lie on your side and perform the rear delt raises one arm at a time. The lying reverse flye is a superior exercise, because it allows for a greater stretch of the posterior deltoid when the dumbbell passes across the chest and comes close to the floor. And unlike conventional bent-over laterals, you have better leverage at the top of the movement, which allows greater contraction in the posterior deltoids.

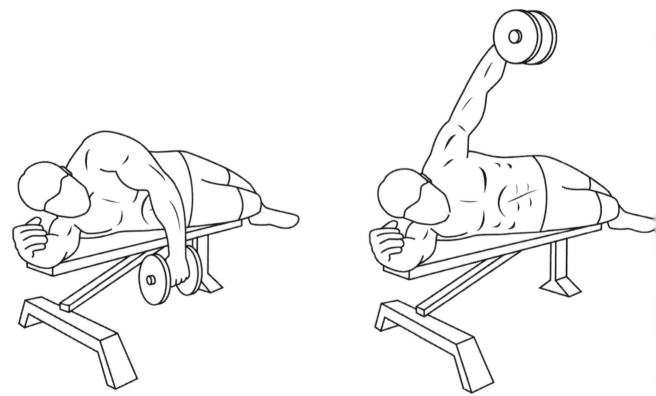

Transverse Abdominus

Most people focus on the six-pack or the rectus abdominus. Yet when it comes to posture and tightening the waist, it's really the unseen transverse abdominus that is important. The transverse abdominus lies underneath the six-pack and is responsible for bringing your stomach in, as well as stabilizing your torso. Thus, when you tighten the transverse abdominus, you instantly have a thinner waist and straightened posture.

One simple exercise that works your transverse abdominus as well postural alignment is known as "the Plank."

Place your hands and feet on the floor as if you were going to perform a pushup. But instead of performing a pushup, simply hold that position for as long as you can. Keep your head, torso and legs straight and aligned with each other. Tighten your abs, triceps, and thighs, and do not let your stomach and hips sag. If they do, then that is the end of the set.

Stretching

With regards to stretching to improve posture, a lot of bodybuilders have overly tight chest muscles. The tight pectorals bring their shoulders in, and so a lot of bodybuilders have a hunched over look.

One way to remedy this is to stretch the pecs with movements like the Doorway Stretch. Simply grab a doorframe with both hands and lean your upper body forward past the frame. Gravity and the weight of your body leaning forward should give you a good stretch in the chest.

"So Easy, A Caveman Can Do It"

If people mistake you for the Geico caveman, then for the love of God, stop the bench pressing and apply the preceding tactics to get rid of the slouch.

XIV. Strong and Ripped: Achieving the Hard-Body

If you're a woman and looking to lose fat and slim down, then your plan is really quite simple: run, diet and yoga or Pilates. But if you're a man, then you're looking to maintain or build muscle AND get ripped. The following are strength training programs that (when coupled with a sound diet and cardio interval training) result not only in fat loss, but will also help retain you muscle mass to give you that ripped, hard body look.

Be warned: these programs are brutally difficult!

8x8

This is the classic "honest workout" by Vince Gironda. Although it was designed to be a muscle-building program, I found it to be a far better fat loss and conditioning program. The premise of 8x8 is simple, although the execution of the program is brutally hard. You simply perform 8 sets of 8 reps of one exercise with only 10-15 second rests. Perform 8 exercises to cover all 8 major muscle groups of the body, and you've got a complete fat loss/strength training program.

Now most people will not be able to perform 8 sets of 8 reps and will fall short of the 64 total reps. Most people cannot handle the 10 second rests at first. When you start out on this program, start with one minute rests, and knock the rest periods down week by week: 45 seconds, 30 seconds, 20 seconds, 15 seconds, and finally 10 seconds. Change the exercises from week to week as well.

The Tabata Method

The Tabata Method is similar to 8x8, but involves the use of timed sets. In the Tabata Method you perform as many reps as you can with a given weight in a 20 second period, rest for 10 seconds, then repeat for 7 more sets. The Tabata Method is an even more difficult version of 8x8, but it has its logistical drawbacks. It is much easier to put your mind and body on autopilot when you know your set and rep goals (8x8). With the Tabata Method, however, you must time your sets (20 seconds) in addition to count and record your reps. Unless you have a training partner, this can slow down the pace of the workout. Not good for a fat loss workout.

EDT

Charles Staley conceived the program EDT or "Escalating Density Training." Just like the aforementioned 8x8 program, although EDT was designed to be something else (a strength building program), I've found it to be a much better fat loss and conditioning program. Just like 8x8, EDT is simple in theory, but brutal in practice.

For EDT choose 2 exercises for different body parts, alternate between them and perform as many reps as you can within a 15-minute period. For your next workout involving these exercises, however, you must beat the previous total of reps. There are no prescribed rest periods and no set or rep recommendations. There is more to this program, but the basic premise is that you dictate the pace of the workout, and increase the density of training from workout to workout.

I have found EDT to be an excellent fat loss/strength training program, but *only* for trainees who are well disciplined and have an iron will. Newbies and undisciplined people do not do well on EDT, because of the lack of structure. Most people just want everything written down in black and white (sets, reps, rest, exercises, etc.), and when you tell them to beat their previous rep total, they simply don't have the drive to do it.

PHA

Perpheral Heart Action (PHA) is the formal name of "circuit training," which was popularized by Mr. America Bob Gajda in the 1960's. PHA involves doing a series of exercises in succession, each exercise emphasizing a different body part. Typically exercises are alternated between the upper body and lower body, and involve the use of machines. A total of 8-9 exercises are chosen to cover the whole body. Because of the liberal use of machines in circuit training, there is greater isolation of the muscles targeted in each exercise, which makes it easier to complete the circuits.

GBC

German Body Composition (GBC) is the brainchild of Charles Poliquin. The gist of GBC involves alternating all of your upper and lower body exercises. Essentially it is a mini version of a circuit, whereby you alternate between only two exercises. For example, you would perform 10-12 reps of squats and then immediately follow it by a set of pushups. Repeat for 2-3 more sets.

The advantage of GBC is that it is easier to execute in the gym than the traditional circuit. Since you are performing only two exercises in succession, you only occupy 1-2 pieces of equipment. With traditional circuit training, however, you may occupy anywhere from 4 to 9 nine workout stations. And if you workout at a commercial gym to do circuit training, you'll just end up pissing a lot of people off.

Complexes

"Complexes" are a series of free weight exercises performed in succession with the same barbell or dumbbell weight in hand. Again, you alternate between upper body and lower body exercises. Essentially complexes are free weight versions of PHA training.

The disadvantage of complexes, however, is that because you are using a free weight which never leaves your hands, you are more likely to fatigue due to weakening grip and you will not complete the complex. This is due to the stabilizer muscles (such as the trapezius) and forearms failing before the prime movers. If you are able to grin and bare it, however, then you will find complexes a very good conditioning method.

Diminishing Sets

100 rep sets or diminishing sets are an excellent way to tap into the slow-twitch muscle fibers, which (unlike fast-twitch muscle fibers) utilize fat as fuel. The goal of diminishing sets is perform a total of 100 reps for an exercise at a given weight in the least amount of sets. As a result, high repetitions (up to 100 of course) are used. Typically, bodyweight exercises are chosen, such as pushups or hyperextensions.

The great thing about diminishing sets is that they can easily be incorporated into a conventional program to not only emphasize fat loss, but active recovery as well.

A Quick Overview of Bodybuilding Diets

A fat loss/strength training program doesn't work, unless you're dieting. This should go without saying, but many people would rather put in an hour a day of disciplined training rather than 24 hours a day of disciplined dieting. Effective fat loss diets have two commonalities:

1. Lower calories (duh!). If you burn more calories than you are taking in, then you will lose weight and hopefully fat. This has always been the case and the supreme rule in weight loss. So eat less.
2. Lower carbohydrate intake. All calories being equal, the more effective fat loss diets revolve around lowering carbohydrate intake, particularly processed carbs. Atkin's, South Beach, the Zone, etc. have all made their mark by emphasizing a lower carbohydrate intake than what was previously recommended.

Having experimented with different diets with myself and with my clients, here are some my observations:

It is easier to think about the categories of foods to eat rather than stressing about counting calories and avoiding particularly dishes or snacks. It is much better to define yourself by what you do or eat rather than define yourself by what you are not or do not eat. Any diet can be implemented the correct way or the wrong way.

For example, the Atkin's diet can be very healthy and effective for fat loss or it can be very unhealthy yet still very effective for fat loss. Atkin's can be very healthy as long as you eat animal proteins (beef, poultry, fish) free from unnatural processes (no hormones, free range, etc), healthy fats (fats containing high concentrations of omega 3's such as fish oil) and lots of green vegetables (which are naturally low carb and high in fiber and phytonutrients).

Atkin's can be very unhealthy, however, if your proteins were primarily processed meats (deli meats, sausages, etc.), and if you ate no vegetables and no healthy fats. I have met people who implemented Atkin's the wrong way and ended up gaunt with bad breath and constant constipation.

Vegetarian diets can also be very healthy or very unhealthy. You can either define the diet by what you should eat (vegetables) or by what you shouldn't eat (meat). I have seen plenty of vegetarians and so-called vegans eat a shitty diet of processed carbs with no raw vegetables. Yet because they're not eating meat, they think they're healthy.

"It's a vegetarian pizza which is healthy, because it has no meat."

Get out of here! If you're a vegetarian, then you have to eat lots of vegetables. They don't call you "anti-meatarians."

For Those Who Want Muscle...

If you are looking to get big and bulk up, then simplify your life and follow 2 rules: eat a lot of calories and eat a lot of protein. Whereas the macronutrient profile of fat loss diets is low carb, moderate to high protein, and moderate to high fat, a muscle gaining diet typically has an equal distribution of macronutrients.

For example, a high calorie Zone diet is the way to go when you want a simple way to maximize muscle gains. The down side of course is that high calorie diets and high animal protein diets will shorten your life span over the long run.

If you've read "The China Study," then you'll know that the higher your ingestion of animal proteins, the greater your chances of getting various life threatening diseases, from cardiovascular disease to diabetes and various cancers. So to live a longer life, it's best to adopt a vegetarian type of diet.

HOWEVER, if you're concerned not just about the length of your life, but the quality of life, the enjoyment of life, and looking muscular while enjoying your life, then you should not limit your protein intake, particularly your animal protein intake. If you want a balance between looking lean and muscular and living a long and healthy life, then a Paleolithic-type of diet is the way to go.

In a Paleo diet, you eat all of the things that would have been readily available to our early hunter-gatherer ancestors. Thus, you would eat a wide variety of animal proteins, as long as they are free range and free from hormone injections. You would also eat a wide variety of organically grown fruits, vegetables and raw nuts.

Processed carbs and meats, however, would be out of the picture. The greater the process or alteration of the food by humans, the more unhealthy it is for you. So although oranges are excellent food choice, a glass of orange juice is not, because it has gone through a process of squeezing out a dozen oranges to create one glass. Your insulin levels would go through the roof if you drank your oranges rather than eating them.

This is also the case with grains, which can be turned into bread (which is at the top of the glycemic index). Rice goes through a long process, and will cause a huge dump of insulin in your body as well. Any food that comes in a box and can be nuked is obviously processed.

If you cannot stick solely to organic meats and produce, then the best thing is to forget about the organic route and stick with a wide variety of unprocessed meats (beef, poultry, fish, etc.), a wide variety of fruits, a wide variety of vegetables and a wide variety of nuts. With the exception of organic yogurt, stay away from dairy (again, it's gone through a process). Eliminate grains and processed carbs such as sugar and starchy carbs such as bread, pastas, potatoes and rice.

If you were taught the four food groups in school, then a simple way to follow the Paleo diet would be to concentrate on eating in the meat/poultry/fish group and the fruit/vegetables group. Minimize your intake of the dairy group, the bread/grains group and of course the junk food group.

To break it all down for you simply even more, just follow 5 dieting tips:

Tip #1: Drink only water, unsweetened tea, or coffee with cream but no sugar. Fruit juices, sodas, milk, sports drinks and alcohol are big no-no's when it comes to getting lean. Stick to one serving (the size of the serving is up to you) of coffee in the morning, and then drink lots and lots of water (at least 8 glasses) and green tea (at least three cups, but not in the evening).

Tip #2: Avoid all starchy carbs such as bread, pasta, noodles, pastries, cereals, potatoes, rice, etc. If you want to see how badly you'll bloat on carbs, just stick a piece of bread in a bowl of water.

Tip #3: Avoid refined sugar.

Tip #4: Eat animal proteins. Eat as much poultry, fish, beef, pork, and eggs as you want. Just avoid meats with heavy sauces or batter, such as fried chicken or BBQ ribs. Sauces and batter have a lot carbs.

Tip #5: Your carbs should only come from vegetables and fruits.

Eat a crap load of green vegetables. Want to be lean, go green!

The following is a sample diet plan:

Breakfast
- scrambled eggs or omelet or however you like to have your eggs
- optional: ham, sausage, or bacon (yes, bacon!)
- coffee with cream, no sugar (you may sweeten with Splenda if desired)

Lunch
- grilled steak or chicken breast salad
- green tea

Snack
- fruit (but no bananas)

Dinner
- salmon with butter
- asparagus or broccoli

Remember the above are only examples. You can pick and choose your foods, just as long as you have a protein portion and vegetable portion to each of your meals.

While gaining muscle is a fun but hard process (eat big, lift big, get big), fat loss is a bitch (eat less, eat cleaner, exercise more). But if you have a sound plan coupled with an iron will, then you can achieve the hard-bodied look.

XV. Five Battle-Tested Strategies for Size and Strength

When you've been in the iron game for 15 years, you learn a thing or two about building muscle. You've researched all of the training theories and techniques, and you try them out on yourself and then your clients. Some techniques and strategies just plain suck, while others work but are not user friendly (i.e. working out two times a day, six days a week).

There are some strategies, however, that are both effective and user friendly. What I present to you are 5 battle-tested strategies for size and strength.

1) The 10 Set Protocol, a.k.a. The Machine Gun Method

This training goes by many names and many variations:

German Volume Training (Charles Poliquin)
10x10, 8x8 and 15x4 (Vince Gironda)
The Bear (Pavel Tsatsouline).

The strategy works like this: choose one exercise (and ONLY one) for each of the muscle groups you want to train and perform many, many, MANY sets of it. You would perform anywhere from 8 to 20 sets of the same exercise, although 10 sets total is typically chosen as the target (hence the name).

This is high volume training at its best. Think of this training like a machine gun: the first few rounds may maim your target, but the next 10 to 15 will obliterate it. If you don't feel your muscles within the first few sets, then you will definitely feel it within the next ten.

Some words of caution: you are more likely to overtrain on high volume (many sets plus many reps) as opposed to high intensity (heavy weight). So employ heavy weight and low reps (3-6) for the Machine Gun Method. If you use higher reps (such as 10), then the total volume would be high and you will overtrain.

Second, employ the machine gun method on only a handful of body parts. If you employed 10-20 sets on every muscle, then you will overtrain from the sheer volume imposed on your nervous system. Instead, employ the "Shotgun Method" of choosing exercises:

2) The Shotgun Method

I'm not a gun nut, but as you can see, I love the gun analogies. In this method, you choose exercises with the biggest bang for the buck. In other words, choose the fewest number of exercises to stimulate the most of amount of muscle.

We're not talking about bench presses or leg presses, where only half of your body is involved. We're talking about total body exercises like the Olympic lifts (clean and press, the snatch, etc.), deadlifts and squats. These are exercises that induce a huge dump of testosterone in your body.

Once you've chosen two or three "shotgun" movements, you'll blast away at them with multiple sets of heavy weight, a la Machine Gun Method. Then you'll follow up with a few sets of "troubleshooting" movements. These are exercises that you choose to address any lagging muscle groups.

The beauty of this strategy is that whenever you employ the shotgun movements, you create an anabolic response in your body lasting a week. Within this week you can follow-up with exercises to take advantage of that pulse of testosterone and develop any muscles you feel need some extra attention.

Here's how a Shotgun Method program looks like:

Workout #1: Shotgun

Clean and press (back, traps, triceps, biceps and deltoids): 8 sets of 3-5 reps, 90 seconds of rest between sets

Pull-ups (back, biceps, forearms, and deltoids): 8 sets of 3-5 reps, 90 seconds of rest between sets

Deadlifts (quadriceps, hamstrings, back, traps, forearms): 8 sets of 3-5 reps, 90 seconds of rest between sets

Workout #2: Troubleshooting

Seated calf raises: 3 sets of 10-12 reps, 1 minute rest
Leg extensions: 3 sets of 10-12 reps, 1 minute rest
Leg curls: 3 sets of 6-8 reps, 1 minute rest
20° dumbbell press: 3 sets of 6-8 reps, 1 minute rest
Seated cable rows: 3 sets of 6-8 reps, 1 minute rest
Dumbbell laterals: 3 sets of 10-12 reps, 1 minute rest
Incline curls: 3 sets of 6-8 reps, 1 minute rest
Lying dumbbell extensions: 3 sets of 6-8 reps, 1 minute rest

3) The Heavy/Light Method

This is a solid strategy to follow in your quest for size and strength. It is simple but complete, versatile and effective. The heavy/light strategy goes like this: perform heavy sets to develop strength and muscular density, then perform light pumping sets to increase blood flow and capillary development. Hence, you develop both sarcomere and scarcoplasmic hypertrophy in your muscles.

The heavy/light method can be performed in many ways:

Consecutive Sets of Heavy/Light- In this variation, you perform a series of heavy sets for a body part, then follow them up with a series of light sets for the same body part. For example:

> Sets 1-4: 4-6 reps
> Sets 5-7: 10-12 reps

You can use the same exercise for both rep ranges or two different exercises.

The Heavy/Light Compound Set- In this variation, you perform a set of low reps and heavy weight for a body part, then immediately perform a set of higher reps with lighter weight with a different exercise targeting the same body part. An example of this would be 6-8 reps for the bench press followed by 10-12 reps of pushups.

Cross Wiring- This is where you intersperse light sets with heavy sets using the same exercise (also known as wave loading or series training) or with different exercises for the same body part. Typically, in cross wiring two exercises, you alternate between a compound movement and an isolation movement:

Set #1- Barbell Military Press, 3-5 reps, 90 seconds rest
Set #2- Dumbbell laterals, 12-15 reps, 90 seconds rest
Repeat three more times

4) Set Extenders

Set extenders are techniques that allow you to go beyond a normal set for given muscle group. Techniques like rest-pause, compound sets, trisets, and descending sets are all set extenders. The reason these techniques work so well is that they allow you to serve two masters: volume and intensity.

Say you perform 4-6 reps at a given weight. The intensity (or weight) is high, but the volume (reps) is low. If you performed 10-12 reps, then the volume would be high, but intensity would be low.

With set extenders, however, you increase both volume and intensity. When you increase both volume and intensity, then you increase muscular hypertrophy.

Let's take **trisets,** for example. Suppose you can do pull-ups, but you can only perform 4-6 reps. You can extend the set for your back by doing a triset such as this:

Pull-ups (4-6 reps)
Lat bar cable rows (6-8 reps)
Wide grip deadlifts (4-6 reps)

Instead of just doing a set of 4-6 reps, you've now done a triset of 14-20 reps for the back. This is a great way to add extra exercises without overextending the length of your workout.

Other set extenders to consider:

Rest-pause. This is an excellent technique for those who are fast-twitch monsters. In other words, if you respond best to heavy weight and have the endurance of a 90-year old man with lung disease, then this technique will help you fully develop your fast-twitch muscle fibers.

To perform a rest-pause set, load up the bar with a really heavy weight, anywhere from 80 to 95% of your 1RM. Perform one rep, then set the bar down and rest for 10-30 seconds at most. Then pick it up and perform another rep. Continue until you reach your desired number of reps within the extended set, which could be anywhere from 5 –10 reps.

Descending sets. Whereas rest-pause works best for fast-twitch muscles, descending sets work best for slow-twitch muscles, such as the lateral head of the deltoids and calves. This technique also works best in a commercial gym, where you can easily implement it on a dumbbell rack or a cable machine. Simply choose a weight, perform a set, then drop the weight and perform another set. Keep dropping weight and performing sets until you reach your desired total number of reps.

Compound sets. This is when you perform two exercises in a row for one body part (which is different from a superset, where you alternate between sets of two body parts). Compound sets can be implemented in two ways:

1. <u>The Post-Exhaust Compound Set</u>- You've heard of the pre-exhaust method. Well, the post-exhaust compound set is the exact opposite. Post-exhaust requires that you perform a multi-joint movement for a body part followed by a single-joint movement for that same body part. An example of this would be a pull-up followed by stiff-arm pulldowns.
2. <u>The Heavy/Light Compound Set</u>- As I mentioned earlier, this is where you perform low reps with heavy weight for one exercise, then immediately perform higher reps with a lighter weight of another exercise. The heavy/light method can be combined with the post-exhaust method: front squats (4-6 reps) followed immediately by leg extensions (10-12 reps).

<u>5) Back Cycling: Controlled Overtraining</u>

"Back cycling" is a training strategy where you purposely overtrain yourself for a short period of time and then pull back to allow your body to overcompensate with muscular growth. Bodybuilders had played around with the concept since the early days, but no one had promoted it as a training strategy until Leo Costa and Russ Horine promoted it in the late 1980's and 1990's.

Back cycling is not the same as "muscle confusion," which is simply a haphazard changing of routines without rhyme or reason. Back cycling is best described as "controlled overtraining."

You purposely increase the *density* of training for a short period of time, anywhere from three days to three weeks. In other words, you do will more work per unit of time. This means increased sets, reps, and exercises per workout, but the workout length will remain the same: 45-60 minutes. To pack in more sets, reps and exercises within this brief time frame, you must employ shorter rest periods and possibly use set extenders as well. Think of it as putting your body into overdrive.

You cannot stay in overdrive forever, though. Go beyond three weeks, and you will overtrain. This is when you have to pull back or "back cycle." Rather than focus on training density, you will decompress the volume and focus on training *intensity*. This means heavier weight, lower reps, higher rest periods and fewer sets and exercises.

Here's a back cycling routine using both the classic 10x10 and 5x5 methods:

Week 1-3 (Density)

10 sets of 10 reps with 1 minute rest periods
One exercise per muscle group
8 muscle groups (Chest, Back, Deltoids, Bicep, Triceps, Quads, Hamstrings, Calves)

Week 4-6 (Decompression)

5 sets of 5 reps with 3 minute rest periods
One exercise per muscle group
5 muscle groups (Chest, Back, Quads, Hamstrings, Calves)

If you look closely, the 10x10 method has greater training density than the 5x5 method. You're doing four times as much volume per muscle group with *shorter* rest periods:

10x10=100 reps vs. 5x5=25 reps

The 5x5 method, however, has greater intensity, since you're focusing on heavier weight with fewer exercises. Despite the greater intensity, you're pulling back from training density by employing longer rest periods (3 minutes).

Plan Your Workout. Work Out to Your Plan.

Now that I've shown you some battle proven strategies for size and strength, go out there, weekend warrior, and kick some ass in the gym.

XVI. The Six Factors of Hypertrophy

There is more than one way to skin the proverbial cat, and with muscle building, this is very true. Most people take a one-dimensional approach to training: lift big; get big.

But there's more to training for size than just heavy weight. The following are the six training factors of hypertrophy:

1) High Intensity – Like I said, most lifters have this base covered. Lift big; get big. Question is, "What constitutes big weight?"

Typically, beginners start with higher reps to practice the movement. Perform 10-12 reps and essentially you are practicing the lift 10-12 times. Newbie lifters respond very well to this rep range, because the exercises are still new to their nervous systems.

Over time, however, a lifter becomes used to the movements. They no longer get sore, and the size and strength gains stop. The optimal hypertrophy zone drops from 10-12 reps to 8-10 to 6-8, and eventually (if they train long enough) 4-6 reps. Ask anyone who's been lifting for a while what their favorite rep range is, and they will quote you a range somewhere within 3-8 reps.

Bottom line: choose an intensity or weight appropriate to your optimal hypertrophy zone.

2) High Volume – Most people think volume refers solely to the number of sets performed, but it is actually the total number of reps performed for a given body part in a given workout. For example: 3 exercises at 3 sets of 6 reps equals to a total volume of 54 reps. The greater the volume, the greater the muscle hypertrophy. The caveat, however, is that you must combine volume with the intensity appropriate for your training age. The

greater the intensity, the greater the number of sets needed to increase the total volume. So while a beginner can perform 3 sets of 10 reps for total volume of 30 reps, an advanced trainee may need to perform 6 sets of 5 reps to reach the same total volume of 30 reps.

3) <u>High Density</u> – While intensity refers to how hard you work and volume refers to how much you work, density refers to how much work you do within a given period of time. Think of high density as more volume in less time. The more reps you perform within a given period of time, the greater your training density. The greater your training density, the greater your muscular hypertrophy. If you find you've hit a plateau, then increasing your training density will help break through any plateaus in size and strength.

4) <u>High Frequency</u> – The more you train, the faster your gains come. This doesn't necessarily mean you'll achieve more hypertrophy, just that you'll achieve it faster and retain it better. It's just like practicing a new skill, like learning a new language. As long as you train correctly, then your body will gain and retain muscle and strength at a faster rate with high frequency training. The caveat, however, is that your training must be short and brief: no more than 45 to 60 minutes a workout. The more often you train, the shorter your training sessions must be. To increase the hypertrophy of a muscle, you should train it at least 3 times a week.

5) <u>High Tension</u> – The greater the muscular tension, the greater the hypertrophy. It is this tension that causes the targeted muscle fibers to thicken up and get bigger. Question is: How do you achieve muscular tension? Obviously we lift weights to create that tension, but not all movements create the same amount of tension or type of tension. Here are three ways to create maximal muscular tension:

1. Heavy weights (duh!) – The greater the weight, the more your muscles have to tense up (hence, tension) to hold or move the weight.

2. Peak contraction movements – These are exercises where the end point of the movement (where full muscle contraction is achieved) is the hardest portion of the movement to perform. Typically, peak contraction movements tend to be cable exercises, since the tension is always high at the end of the exercise's range of motion.

3. Stretch movements – These are exercises where the starting point of the movement stretches the muscle being worked. This stretching not only creates a lot tension on the muscle, but it also causes the muscle to release localized hormones (such as IGF and FGF) that incur hypertrophy. Examples of stretch movements include flyes and incline curls.

<u>6) Wide variety</u> – People talk about mind-numbing boredom, but your muscles get bored too. This is why when it comes to exercises, your muscles prefer a wide variety of them at different angles and on different apparatuses (free weights, cables, bodyweight, etc.). This does not mean, however, that you include all of your favorite exercises in one workout. A lot people go crazy and include 5 different exercises for the chest in a single workout. That's overkill. Your body responds better if you simply rotate exercises from workout to workout.

Apply these six factors in your program design, and you've built a complete hypertrophy routine.

- .
- .
- .
- .

What's that? You want me to give you a program applying these six factors? I guess that's why you bought the book, because you want it all laid out for you. The program is appropriately titled "The 6 Factors Program."

Workout #1

Quads Triset:
Front squats (4) 5-7 reps
Sissy squats (4) AMRAP
Leg extensions (4) 10-12 reps,
2:00

Chest Compound Set:
20° DB press (4) 5-7 reps
Pushups (4) AMRAP, 2:00

Triceps Compound Set:
Lying EZ-bar extensions (4) 5-7
reps
Lying dumbbell extensions (4) 5-7
reps, 4:00

Workout #2

Back Triset:
Pull-ups (4) AMRAP
Pullovers (4) 5-7 reps
Stiff-arm pulldowns (4) 10-12
reps, 3:00

Deltoid Triset:
Wide grip upright rows (3) 10-12
reps
Prone incline laterals (3) 10-12
reps
Swing laterals (3) 10-12 reps,
2:00

Biceps Triset:
Incline hammer curls (3) 5-7 reps
Standing dumbbell curls (3) 5-7
reps
Lying cable curls (3) 5-7 reps,
2:00

Calves Diminishing Sets:
One legged calf raises – 100 reps,
bodyweight only, alternate
between legs with no rest

Workout #3

Hack squats (3) 8-12 reps, 1:30
Good mornings (3) 8-12 reps, 1:30
Guillotine press (3) 8-12 reps,
1:30
Close grip pulldowns (3) 8-12
reps, 1:30
Lying dumbbell curls (3) 8-12
reps, 1:00
Elevated diamond pushups (3)
AMRAP, 1:00
Rear laterals (3) 8-12 reps, 1:00
One legged calf raises (3) AMRAP,
1:00

Workout #4

Back squats (6) 3-5 reps, 2:00
Bench press (6) 3-5 reps, 2:00
Seated close grip cable rows (6) 4-
6 reps, 2:00
Calves Descending Sets:
Dumbbell calf raises (2) each set
consists of 5 drop set with 8-12
reps each drop set, 2:00

Additional notes:

- AMRAP stands for "as many reps as possible"
- Numbers in parentheses () refer to number of sets
- Times indicate length of rest between sets, trisets, and compound sets
- Choose weights appropriate for the rep ranges indicated

This program applies all 6 factors of hypertrophy. It is a four day per week program with 3 different types of workouts. Each of these workouts either sensitizes your body to or maximizes your body's output of the major anabolic hormones: growth hormone, testosterone, and insulin.

The GH Workouts

Workouts 1 and 2 are designed to maximize your output of growth hormone. The workouts do this by utilizing set extenders such as compound sets and trisets. Set extenders such as these increase training density, which leads to an increased GH output as well as moderate testosterone output.

The Insulin/Testosterone Sensitizing Workout

Workout 3 is a full body workout designed to sensitize your body to the anabolic effects of insulin and testosterone. It does this by employing higher reps (for insulin sensitization) and high tension movements (for testosterone receptivity).

The Testosterone Boosting Workout

Workout #4 is a full body workout designed to maximize your body's output of testosterone. It does this by employing heavy compound movements. In this instance, the power bodybuilding approach is used to recruit as many muscle fibers throughout the body. These heavy compound movements elicit a huge testosterone jolt from you body.

Follow this program for two weeks only. Afterwards you'll follow a decompression workout of your choice. In other words, take it easy: hold off on the set extension techniques, rest longer between sets (2-3 minutes), *and no more than 3-4 sets per body part.*

Whereas you must go balls to the walls during the two weeks of the Six Factors Program, you must pull back from the workload during decompression week. Don't perform more than one exercise per body part. After your decompression week, you can come back to the program and repeat the cycle as often as you'd like.

When you come back to the Six Factors Program, you can substitute exercises as long as you follow the rep, set, and rest protocols outlined. You must also adhere to the requirements of each workout. Workouts 1 and 2 require you to use set extenders such compound sets and trisets. Workout 3 requires high reps and high tension movements. Workout 4 requires the Shotgun Method: employing the minimum number of heavy compound exercises to cover most of the body.

When you take a day or two off between workouts is up to you. Just complete all four days within a week and do not perform 3 workouts in a row.

This program is not for beginners or for half-ass lifters. You must be an intermediate to advanced lifter to attempt this program. Obviously, you should be eating a lot of food, a lot of protein, drinking a lot of water, and getting a lot of quality sleep.

This program is insanely tough and yet immensely rewarding. Follow the 6 Factors Program, and you will be amazed by the results.

Recommended Reading

There you have it: a wealth of bodybuilding principles, strategies and programs designed to give the most muscle for your efforts. Your search for knowledge should not end here, of course. This is by no means the be all and end all of bodybuilding books. Here is a list of my influences, and I suggest you immerse yourself in the writings of these bodybuilding and strength coaches:

Vince Gironda

No other man has had such an influence on bodybuilding training and dieting. NO ONE. Virtually every bodybuilding strategy and tactic that you see in the gym today can be traced back to Vince. Do you follow a pyramid program of 10-8-6 and then follow up with a flushing set of 15? Guess what? Vince popularized that. Low carb dieting to get you ripped to the bone? Yep, Vince came up with that long before Atkins. Getting fantastic results from doing the Tabata method? Vince came up with 8x8 to make grown men cry long before any of that research came out on 10 second rests and its effect on strength and fat loss.

But Vince's forte was coming up with exercises that created a lot of tension on a targeted muscle. He had an artist's understanding of how certain exercises could develop a particular look and develop a physique that was pleasing to the eye, not grotesque. When it came down to it, Vince understood both the science of training and dieting and the art of bodybuilding.

Serious Growth Series

This series of books had the most influence on my training than any other. The books didn't just provide training programs, they provided the reader with an understanding of how to choose and create programs. The Serious

Growth Series created a true bodybuilding paradigm. Authors Leo Costa Jr. and Russ Horine smashed a lot of sacred cows during the 80's and 90's:

- Instead of training a body part once or twice a week, they proposed training a body part at minimum three times a week
- They pushed the idea of 45 minute time limits to workouts, at a time when trainees slaved away in the gym for a couple of hours

What distinguished their bodybuilding training paradigm from all others was the utilization of overtraining as a viable means to gain muscle in the long run. This concept of cycling between phases of overtraining and "hyperadaptation" was truly revolutionary and one of the best-kept secrets in bodybuilding. The reason it is one of the best-kept secrets is that very few people have the smarts and guts to train on the way they propose

Michael Gundhill

This author is unknown to most people, but he published a series of insightful articles in Ironman Magazine back in the 1990's. Most of the science investigating weight training focuses on strength development. Michael Gundhill, however, took a look at how different types of weight training elicited different hormonal responses in your body and how these hormones contribute to muscular hypertrophy.

Charles Poliquin

This strength coach extraordinaire revived the science of bodybuilding. Poliquin took what worked in the science of strength and applied it to hypertrophy training in bodybuilding. What marked his applications different from the applications of other strength coaches to bodybuilding was his idea of fiber-type training. People with primarily fast-twitch muscles now understood a better method to gain muscle than the standard 8-12 reps.

Pavel Tsatsouline

Be big and strong like Russian bear, comrade! Ex-Soviet military Pavel Tsatsouline infused new interest in functional bodybuilding, the idea that a muscular physique should be a side effect of strength and function and not the primary goal. Part of Pavel's appeal is his ability to explain rather complex physiological processes with simple and clear language and logic.

The Strength and Physique Blog

And of course, you can always read my thoughts as a personal trainer at my blog:

www.strengthandphysique.blogspot.com

I always enjoy hearing from my readers, so shoot me an email or post a comment on the blog.

As always, train smart and stay safe.

JC

Made in the USA